# PARALEGAL TRAINING MANUAL

# PARALEGAL TRAINING MANUAL

### Deborah E. Larbalestrier

*Legal Assistant*
*Litigation and Workmen's Compensation Specialist*
*Executive Director of the American Paralegal Association*

**PRENTICE-HALL, INC.**

**ENGLEWOOD CLIFFS, NEW JERSEY**

Prentice-Hall International, Inc., *London*
Prentice-Hall of Australia, Pty. Ltd., *Sydney*
Prentice-Hall of Canada, Ltd., *Toronto*
Prentice-Hall of India Private Ltd., *New Delhi*
Prentice-Hall of Japan, Inc., *Tokyo*
Prentice-Hall of Southeast Asia Pte. Ltd., *Singapore*
Whitehall Books, *Wellington, New Zealand*

© 1981 by

Prentice-Hall, Inc.
Englewood Cliffs, N.J.

*"This publication is designed to provide accurate and authoritative
information in regard to the subject matter covered. It is sold with the
understanding that the publisher is not engaged in rendering legal,
accounting, or other professional service. If legal advice or other
expert assistance is required, the services of a competent professional
person should be sought."*

—*From the Declaration of Principles jointly adopted by a
Committee of the American Bar Association and a Committee
of Publishers and Associations.*

**Library of Congress Cataloging in Publication Data**

Larbalestrier, Deborah E.
    Paralegal training manual.

    Includes index.
    1. Legal assistants—United States—Handbooks,
manuals, etc.   I. Title.
KF319.L26              347.73′504′0202           81-5054
ISBN   0-13-648626-6        347.3075040202         AACR2

Printed in the United States of America

# A Word from the Author

This on-the-job training manual includes everything that has taken legal assistants working in the field many years to learn through tried and proven on-the-job performance. Hence, no matter what field of law your attorney has as his specialty, this concise, training manual will provide you with the knowledge you need to become a top-notch. competent, viable member of the legal team. The manual not only tells you *what to do* as it relates to step-by-step procedures, but in most instances, it also tells you *how to do it* in clear, straightforward terms.

The objectives of the book are to have as a ready finger-tip reference, basic step-by-step procedures as to the following: how to prepare legal documents; how to do legal research; preparing cases for trial for your attorney, and the like. One or two representative forms for each type of legal procedure are included so that you can get some idea of what these forms look like. For other forms, you are referred to the standard state and local form books available in your office.

Characteristically, you will find tried and proven solutions to problems and step-by-step procedures such as;

- How to Conduct the Initial Client Interview;
- How to Draft a Complaint;
- How to Prepare an Answer;
- How to Authenticate Documents;
- How to Obtain Documents from Witnesses;
- How to Prepare Office Files;
- Step-By-Step Procedures for Filing a Civil Lawsuit;
- Step-By-Step Procedure for Handling a Criminal Case from Arrest to Trial;

- A Checklist to Help You Administer an Intestate or Testate Probate Proceeding;
- A Checklist or Guide in Setting up a Corporation or Other Corporate Entity;
- If anticipated that the case will go to trial, when to File a Demand for Jury Trial;
- In anticipation of a default, how to prepare the necessary documents;
- How to develop Interrogatories;
- How to develop Requests for Admissions; and more.

In short, this book will enable you to enhance your productivity on-the-job expeditiously and efficiently.

**Deborah E. Larbalestrier**

# ACKNOWLEDGMENT

A special thanks to my friend and supervising litigation specialist, Linda Bever, whose cooperation in supplying me with material and suggestions for the litigation section cannot be measured in words.

This same appreciation goes to my boss, Edward B. Mills, an attorney specializing in criminal law, who aided me in supplying the forms needed for the criminal law section.

This book could not be a nationally oriented book without the assistance of those legal assistants and law firms in the States of Indiana, Missouri, New York, Oregon, Florida and Texas. A grateful and sincere thanks to all of you.

Deborah E. Larbalestrier

Litigation Specialist,
Executive Director,
American Paralegal Association

# TABLE OF CONTENTS

**Functional Duties During Litigation,** *(continued)*

Process  •  Preparing Your Brief (Personal
Observation  •  Self-Analysis  •  Practical
Hint)  •  Preparing Your Exhibits (Helpful
Hint  •  Introduction to Forms  •  Sample Forms)

Introduction  •  Step-by-Step Procedures
(Pitfalls)  •  Shepardizing (Step-by-Step
Procedure)  •  Sample Memoranda (in Support of
Motion for Partial Summary Judgment  •  in Support of
Demurrer)

Introduction  •  Plaintiff's Procedure in the Discovery
Process (Interrogatories  •  Request for
Admissions)  •  Defendant's Procedure in the
Discovery Process (Interrogatories  •  Request for
Admissions)  •  Deposition—Procedure as to Both
Litigants  •  Discovery—Digesting the Deposition
(Purpose  •  Checklist in Preparing a Deposition
Summary)  •  Enforcement Orders
(Depositions  •  Interrogatories  •  Summary of a
Paraprofessional's Functional Duties in the Area of
Discovery)  •  Production of Documents—Notice and
Motion (How Do You Obtain These
Documents?  •  Step-by-Step Practical
Procedures  •  The VIP Pleading)  •  Physical and
Mental Examination—Notice and Motion (Procedure for
Filing Motion)  •  Sample Interrogatory  •  Twelve
Sample Objections to Interrogatories  •  Sample
Request for Admission  •  Sample Depositions

**Working with the Rules of Evidence,** *(continued)*

the Weight of Evidence  •  Establishing and Proving a
Prima Facie Case in Replevin (Step-by-Step
Procedure)  •  Establishing Prima Facie Evidence on an
Insurance Policy Claim  •  Unlawful Detainer
Action  •  Establishing a Prima Facie Case in a
Contract Claim  •  Sample Forms

Introduction  •  Doctrines Affecting
Liability  •  Liabilities of the Parties
Determined  •  What Are the Defenses to These
Liabilities?  •  Other Liabilities You Should Be Aware
of  •  Defenses to a Products Liability
Case  •  Checklist for Working with a Casualty Claim
or Tort Action  •  The Medical Malpractice Defense
(Establishing Violations of Duties  •  Legal Doctrines
Affecting Medical Malpractice  •  Step-by-Step
Procedure)  •  Filing a Claim Against a Municipality or
Other Legal Entity  •  Working with a Personal
Injury-Property Damage Action

Checklists in Working with Family Law Matters
(Preparing the Ante-Nuptial Agreement  •  Alimony
and Child Support  •  Enforcing Support
Orders)  •  Checklist for Determining Source of
Community Property  •  Checklist for Completing
Family Law Forms (as Used in
California)  •  Functional Duties of the Legal
Assistant  •  Sample Forms

**Working with a Contract Transaction,** *(continued)*

of Particulars  •  Pleading Actions in Equity (Defenses
Which Can Be Pleaded)  •  Dealing with Statutes
(Sample Complaint)

Introduction  •  Timesaver Hints  •  Pre-Hearing
Step-by-Step Procedure  •  Examination of Judgment
Debtor (Documents Prepared Before
Examination  •  Documents to Be Prepared After
Examination  •  Documents Which May Be Prepared
in a Contempt Proceedings)  •  Step-by-Step Procedure Re:
Enforcing Judgment in Other States  •  Step-by-Step
Procedure for Execution (Issuance of Writ of
Mandamus  •  Levy on Property  •  Sale)  •  Rights and
Remedies of Judgment Debtor  •  Checklist Re
Judgments (Judgment Enforceable by
Execution  •  Property Subject to
Execution)  •  Checklist for Priorities

Introduction  •  Interviewing the Accused (Basic
Questions to Ask  •  Pertinent Questions About the
Client  •  Step-by-Step Procedure: Arrest to Trial to
Appeal)  •  Definitive Step-by-Step Procedures
Post-Trial to Appeal  •  Introduction to Forms
(Samples of Forms)

Things to Remember (Special Problems  •
Special Statutory Periods  •  Costs of Registering

**Working with Copyright Registrations and
  Trademarks,** *(continued)*

Copyright Claims   •   Costs of Recording Documents)
•   Trademarks   •   Trade Names (Basic Elements)
•   Suggested Defenses to the Infringement of a Trade
Name   •   Trade Secrets   •   Elements to Include in a
Complaint for Unfair Competition Based on a ''Trade
Secret''   •   Definition/Comparison Checklist

# PARALEGAL
# TRAINING
# MANUAL

# The
# Interview

*Remember: A paralegal can give "legal information" not "legal advice."*

# CHAPTER 1

## INTRODUCTION

In some offices, the policy may be to have the initial interview of all new cases done by the attorney, then referred by him to his legal assistant in the presence of the client. However, your attorney may have advised the client that his legal assistant would be working with him on the case and had obtained his permission to have you present during the interview.

It is the trend in some offices today to have the legal assistant do the initial interviewing, with a subsequent referral to the attorney for a more in-depth consultation at a later date. The purpose of this procedure could be to await receipt of more initial information from the client; or the receipt of preliminary investigative reports.

*Note*, that there is no black or white procedure in the interviewing process. It is a matter of office policy. As long as you know the boilerplate procedures of the interviewing process, you will be able to adapt to any office policy.

What is important is that you establish immediately a good rapport with the client. Then, and only then, can you commence to gather the facts. Remember, **be patient; a client does not know what is and what is not important.** At the time of the interview he may be distraught and in trouble. Otherwise, he would not be in your attorney's office seeking legal advice. For these reasons, he may digress, so you must be firm and in control of the interview.

21

You are cautioned NEVER, NEVER GIVE LEGAL ADVICE.

Consider the following: LEGAL ADVICE, as we understand the phrase, is the giving of information leading to the planning of strategy in the prosecution of a claim which utilizes an attorney's analytical and judgmental abilities based on interpretation of the law applicable to a given set of facts.

LEGAL INFORMATION is the giving of information which is of public record and can be found in any statute or code book applicable to a given set of facts, and may include general principles of law.

The latter is all that you, as a legal assistant, can give to a client. UNDER NO CONDITIONS should you attempt to explain legal rights. UNDER NO CONDITIONS should you advise a client what he can and cannot do—this is planning strategy.

You can tell the client about the statute of limitations problem, or what the statute of limitations period is. And, you can tell the client how to complete a Department of Motor Vehicles form such as the SR-1 or the SR-4, but UNDER NO CONDITIONS should you advise the client what he can or cannot do to avoid having his license suspended or revoked. In other words, your function at the interview is to explain procedures, answer questions that are of public record, gather facts; and leave the legal determination and judgment to the attorney.

### FOR EXAMPLE:

*Client:* "What are the legal ramifications if I should file an application for a work-related injury? I do not want to file a lawsuit against my employer. He might fire me."

*Legal Assistant:* "If you mean by ramification what will happen as a result of your filing an application before the Worker's Compensation Appeals Board, this is a matter you should discuss with my boss. I can only tell you that under the law, all employers are required to carry Worker's Compensation insurance to cover injuries to their employees while in the course and scope of their employment."

### OR

*Client:* "I was involved in an automobile accident six months ago and was told that I should seek an attorney to protect my interests. Am I too late?"

*Legal Assistant:* "No, you are not too late. The law states that you have one year from the date of the accident in which to file a personal injury claim. So you have come to our office in a timely manner."

*Client:* "How much money do you think I can get, and what are we going to do to make Mr. Jones pay me for all my pain and suffering?"

*Legal Assistant:* "Mr. Smith, you are now discussing how my boss plans to negotiate and prosecute your claim. I cannot answer these questions, since they are within the bailiwick of the attorney and constitute giving legal advice and planning strategy. I suggest that you wait until your conference with him to discuss these matters. In any event, I will note them on my interview sheet and bring them to his attention."

## Step-by-Step Procedures After the Interview

The following procedures and/or duties of a legal assistant during litigation address themselves to steps taken after you, the legal assistant, have been delegated the responsibility of holding the initial interview with the client.

1. After the interview, immediately dictate (or type) a memorandum to the file (with a copy to your attorney) as to the factual situation;

2. Note with clarity and specificity questions raised by the client for the attorney's attention and response;

3. What, if anything, you told the client relative thereto:

4. What, if anything, is missing and what you have done or will be doing to obtain such pertinent missing documents, etc.:

5. State your feeling about the client (was he nervous, distraught, did you get the feeling he was lying or leaving out something, etc.);

6. Most important, advise the attorney of any statute of limitations problem, if applicable. Note the same on the outside of the file and, of course, on your follow-up calendar;

7. Send out letters of representation to all parties involved, if applicable;

8. Start the investigative process, if applicable;

9. After discussion with your attorney, draft a memorandum of points and authorities applicable to the factual situation;

10. Draft a complaint, if applicable, and hold it in the file until advised by your attorney to have it typed in final form; and

11. When the complaint is filed, after receipt of the answer to complaint (or during and within the statutory period allowed in your state) start your discovery proceeding, if applicable, at the instance and request of your attorney.

A sample interview sheet follows:

CONSIDER THE FOLLOWING FORMS, despite the fact that each office may have its own interview and/or intake sheet:

ATTORNEY IN CHARGE: _____
DATED: _____
ATTORNEY HANDLING: _____

BOOKKEEPING INFORMATION

1. FEE ARRANGEMENT
    [Contingent] _____
    [Retainer] _____
    [Other] _____
2. CHARGE
    [Client] _____
    [Other] _____
    _____
    _____
    _____

CLIENT: (Name) _____
        (Address) _____
        _____
    (Telephone) _____ (Home)
                _____ (Work)
DESCRIPTION OF MATTER: _____
_____
_____
_____

OTHER PARTY: (Name) _____
             (Address) _____
             _____
    (Telephone) _____
OPPOSING COUNSEL: (Name) _____
                  (Address) _____
                  _____
    (Telephone) _____
SPECIAL INSTRUCTIONS: _____
_____
_____
_____

COPIES TO: BOOKKEEPING __ DOCKET _____ FILES _____

## INTERVIEW

### Legal Assistant/Client Suggested Interview

Depending on office policy and for your use in the interviewing process, consider the following examples of tried and proven interviewing procedures:

### SAMPLE A

*Attorney:* Mr. Smith, I would like you to meet Debbie, my legal assistant whom I have asked to work on your file with me. She is well-qualified to do the preliminary interview, and will be doing some of the investigation on my behalf, as well as drafting some of the court pleadings for my review and convenience.

*Client:* How do you do, Debbie?

*Attorney:* As a convenience to you, if at any time I am not in the office when you call, you can always talk to Debbie, who, in turn, will advise me of your concerns; and, if she cannot help you, be assured that I will call you back.

*Client:* That's fine. I hope I won't bother you too much, Debbie, but this lawsuit is making me nervous. I've never been involved in legal matters before.

*Debbie:* That's all right, that's what I'm here for.

### OR
### SAMPLE B

*Attorney:* Mr. Smith, I would like to have my legal assistant sit in on the initial interview after our consultation, if it is all right with you. He is a competent person, well-qualified to assist me in processing your claim.

*Client:* Well, I don't know ...

*Attorney:* Don't worry, he is tight-lipped and understands the fiduciary relationship between the attorney and client, so you can be as open in front of him, as you would be with me.

*Client:* Well, if you think it is okay, I don't care.

*Attorney:* Fine. You'll see, you will like the arrangement, particularly, since you will know that you can talk to him when you call, if I am not in the office. He'll be able to bring you up-to-date on what we are doing or answer any of the questions you may have at the time.

*Client:* Fine.

### OR

## SAMPLE C

*Legal Assistant:* My name is Debbie, and I am Mr. Jones's legal assistant. I will be working with Mr. Jones on your file. He has asked me to handle the initial interview. We will be filling out the interview sheet and other preliminary documents needed for use in investigating your claim.

*Client:* That's fine with me, but I didn't know Mr. Jones used a legal assistant. Is a legal assistant the same as a paralegal? I have heard that term.

*Legal Assistant:* Yes. I've been with Mr. Jones for several years now.

*Client:* Are you an attorney?

*Legal Assistant:* No, I'm not.

*Client:* What do you do for Mr. Jones?

[Here you would describe briefly some of the tasks you perform for your attorney. DO NOT GO INTO MINUTE DETAIL.]

*Client:* That's very interesting. Tell me, what do you think my chances are in winning this case?

*Legal Assistant:* I cannot answer that, you will have to discuss that portion of your case with Mr. Jones.

*Client:* Okay, but can you tell me if it is too late for me to bring an action in this matter? I know I have waited an inordinate amount of time before seeking out a legal advisor in this matter.

*Legal Assistant:* No, I don't believe so. Let's see. The accident occurred on October 28, 1980, and today is August 27, 1981. The statute will run on October 27, 1981, and the Code book says you have one year plus within which to file an action. So, it would appear that you have about two months, or at least two months, three weeks and four or five days in which to file a lawsuit. It is possible to file a lawsuit almost immediately if that is Mr. Jones's desire. But that will be up to him. I will bring this statute matter to Mr. Jones's attention. You might call this afternoon, say about 4:30, and Mr. Jones may have made a decision as to the procedure … etc.

# CHAPTER 2

# Handling the Complaint from Inception to Trial

*This chapter puts into a nutshell what constitutes a good cause of action and refreshes your memory as to the steps in preparing, filing, and defending the same.*

## INTRODUCTION

As you know, in civil practice, as opposed to criminal practice, a complaint is the first pleading to be filed on the part of the plaintiff. It is a concise statement of the facts constituting the cause of action, with each material allegation stated succinctly and numbered separately. The purpose of a complaint is to give the defendant information of all material facts upon which the plaintiff relies to support his demand and cause of action.

As a general proposition, in your State Courts,[1] a complaint sets forth all of the facts known to the plaintiff, as well as incorporating allegations of fact. However, under Rule 8(a) of the Federal Rules of Civil Procedure, the general rule for complaints is that the complaint should contain both a short and plain statement of the claim, showing that the pleader is entitled to relief, and the demand for judgment for the relief to which he deems himself entitled. In federal cases, it should be noted that the complaint should also contain a short and plain statement of the grounds upon which jurisdiction depends.

You are cautioned, however, that since the purpose of any complaint or petition filed on behalf of the plaintiff is to present his story to the court, it should not contain or set forth any possible defenses to any

---

[1]A State Court complaint can also incorporate, by reference, certain documented evidentiary facts which can be proven with testimony by a later production of documents at the time of trial.

29

allegations contained in the complaint. In other words, do not do the work of the defendant or educate him.

The exception to the above, of course, is the pleading of the statute of limitations and the statute of frauds. If these are pleaded, they must appear on the face of the complaint if the defendant is expected to respond and answer same; otherwise, the complaint will fail and a demurrer will be sustained.

*Note*: In the State of California, we have the demurrer which is replaced by a Motion to Dismiss under the Federal Rules of Civil Procedure, and this same practice is prevalent in those states which have adopted this or a similar procedure.

If you are incorporating by reference "a document," be doubly sure that the allegations in the complaint referring to the document are "word-by-word," "line-by-line" quotations from the document, since the slightest deviation will, at the very least, subject your complaint or portion thereof to a general or special demurrer. If this should happen, the document would control.

*Note*: The worst that could happen is that the contradictory allegations in the complaint would be subject to a Motion to Strike. The fatal blow would be a Motion to Strike the entire complaint.

Finally, it is accepted practice that a plaintiff, in order to establish a cause of action, may be required to state facts of which he has no direct personal knowledge. Should this happen, you can allege such facts as follows:

1. "Plaintiff is informed and believes, and based upon such information and belief, alleges ..."; or,

2. "Plaintiff does not possess sufficient information or belief, and based upon such lack of information and belief...."

When it comes to determining what counts should be incorporated in a complaint (counts being the legal theories upon which you based the wrong or breach of duty), it is suggested that you confer with your attorney since he is the one who will have to argue the case in court. Your counts would be such theories as:

(a) Negligence
(b) Intentional tort
(c) Breach of contract, and so forth.

Your initial work is done, if you are the plaintiff, and at this point in the litigation, you start thinking about discovery.

*Note*: But remember, that investigation and discovery may precede service of the complaint on the defendant. There are, of course, limitations on discovery until after the defendant has been served and has had an opportunity to answer. In the event the defendant does not answer, it is possible he has not been served. You should therefore check periodically with your process server to determine when and if the defendant has been served with a copy of the complaint.

Should the defendant not answer in a timely manner (10 days, 30 days—whatever the statutory requirement), you of course, can file for a judgment based on default of the defendant in failing to answer the Complaint within the statutory limitation period.

## IN A NUTSHELL

### What to Incorporate in the Complaint

    I. The Facts
       A. Ultimate Fact
          1. Conclusions of Law
          2. Evidentiary Facts
          3. Effect of the Above.
    II. The Allegations
       A. Information and Belief
       B. No Direct or Personal Knowledge
       C. Expert Opinions
       D. Lack of Actual or Constructive Knowledge
    III. The Cause of Action
       A. Theories
       B. Counts
    IV. Defenses
       A. Statute of Fraud
       B. Statute of Limitation
    V. Incorporation by Reference
       A. Counts Within the Same Pleading
       B. Pleadings Within the Same Case
   VII. Prayer
  VIII. Verification

## PROCESSING THE SUMMONS

The heading and caption on the Summons should be spelled out in a precise manner as on the Complaint. The exception to this rule applies when you have a long list of defendants. In this instance, it is permissible to set forth all of the defendants that your office represents, or you can just name the first-named defendant and then follow that name with the phrase, "et al."

### Key Office Procedure

When the original Complaint and Summons is filed with the court, once the Clerk of the Court has placed the court stamp thereon, with the date the Complaint was filed, and the court number, you should immediately conform all copies by filling in the number of the case which has been assigned, the date of filing, and the Clerk's name, on all of your extra copies—THEN, AND ONLY THEN, serve a copy of the Summons and Complaint on each defendant named.

> *Caution:* Be aware that in many jurisdictions this service upon defendants is accomplished *only* with "Leave of Court" first being had and obtained. You are therefore cautioned to check your local court rules for this procedure.

### Service of Summons

Personal service must be made when possible. If it is not possible, then service may be made by publication, and must be made and returned within the statutory limitation as prescribed by law. (You are cautioned to check your local statutes for this statutory period.)

Additionally, in some jurisdictions, service of Summons may be authorized to be made by certified mail, with return receipt requested. Check your local court rules regarding this procedure.

> *Precautionary Measure:* Fictitious-named defendants must be served with a copy of the Summons with the following notation:
>
> "You are hereby served in the within action as the person named herein as 'DOE 1'."
>
> In other words, you must type this phrase on the copy of the Summons.

Because of the requirement for personal service upon the defendant, the original Summons must be shown to each party-defendant served when serving a copy of the Summons and Complaint; and a Summons must be served within five (5) years from the date of filing of the Complaint. (Check your local statutes for this time limitation.)

*Security Measure:* Finally, after each defendant has been served, you then file the original Summons with the court for safekeeping. The reason for this is that despite all your efforts, the original Summons sometimes gets lost or misfiled and/or mislaid in a stack of court filings; or it simply gets lost by the process server, Marshal, etc.

## Parties

Personal service may also be made by the Sheriff, Constable, Marshal or private party over the age of eighteen (18) years, who is not a party of the action, by handing a copy of the Summons and Complaint to the defendant. It is usually a good procedure for the person serving to state what the document is, i.e., Complaint for Personal Injury, Complaint for Divorce, etc.

Where applicable, and as provided by statute, service on minors under the age of fourteen (14) years may be made as long as there is a legally named guardian involved in the lawsuit and the service can be made upon such guardian—this can be his parent, his aunt, uncle, or any adult with whom he resides, or by whom he is employed.

Minors over fourteen (14) years of age can be personally served without the necessity of serving the named adult or legal guardian.

When serving an incompetent person, you can serve the incompetent, but you must also serve the Guardian ad Litem; or legal guardian, or conservator, etc. These latter-named individuals could be the State or other corporate entity, as well as an individual natural person.

## Proof of Service

If the Sheriff, Marshal, Constable or individual makes the service, he must file a Certificate or Affidavit of Service which is on the reverse side of the Summons: or, on a separate printed form, or one that has been typed up; or, in lieu thereof, a written admission or acknowledgment of service by the defendant. Any typed form must contain the complete caption of the case and court number assigned; and be signed (notarized if out of State), or declared under penalty or perjury.

## For Your Information

"DOES": This is an all-inclusive word for any defendant not presently known, or who may hereafter be found to be a party to the action. As a result, this word must be on the Summons as well as on the Complaint, otherwise, it will fail.

### EXAMPLE:

In a hit-and-run accident, you would, of necessity, be suing a fictitious-named person as the "DOE." Later on, should you ascertain the name of the driver of a hit-and-run vehicle, he could then be served as "DOE I." You would now be in a position to amend your Complaint to assert his true identity and capacity.

During the interim period, however, you have "reserved" the right to serve him by naming him as a "DOE" in the caption of your Complaint, and on the Summons.

*Note*: Under the Federal Rule, there is no provision for the joinder of "DOE" defendants. See *Molner v. N.B.C.* (9th Cir. 1956) 231 *et seq* 684. A pleader who carries over the State practice into the drafting of a Federal complaint may cause himself serious jurisdictional difficulties in a diversity case. The Ninth Circuit has held that a complaint which names "Doe" defendants fails to establish diversity jurisdiction even though it contains allegations that all the defendants are of different citizenship from the plaintiff.

## DEFENDING THE LAWSUIT

If you are the defendant in the litigation, consider the following step-by-step procedures.

When a Complaint comes into your office, you should immediately do the following:

1. Set up a file and index card, and if applicable, obtain an extension of time to answer.

    (a) Calendar it on your follow-up calendar.

    (b) Place it in the appropriate docket book.

2. Examine the complaint to determine if a routine answer, general denial or affirmative defenses are needed, such as contributory negligence or statute of limitations, and advise your attorney.

3. Examine the proof of service (reverse side of Summons) to determine if proper service was made, and if not, whether you can file a Motion to Strike or Special Demurrer or other similar type of document, and advise your attorney.

4. If you find that you can file a simple answer, then draft such a document, attach it to the file and give it to your attorney.

5. If the complaint has more than one cause of action, it is always best to determine the theory under which they are being alleged, i.e., common count, alter ego, breach of contract, and the like. This will aid you in stating your affirmative defenses, after discussion with your attorney.

6. Should you receive a set of interrogatories, review it by comparing the answers, studying the evasions and lack of responses. Flag these for your attorney to be discussed later with the view of filing a Motion to Produce or Compel Further Answers. This, because your attorney may want to object to some of the interrogatories being propounded.

7. At this point, your attorney might also want to file some Requests for Admissions, which admissions would be based upon the plaintiff's answers to the interrogatories propounded, statements of witnesses or testimony of witnesses taken at a deposition; or information which was obtained as a result of a Motion to Produce Documents.

8. If the above is implemented, the next step will be to move for an order that certain facts be admitted. If the plaintiff is allowed to file a response to this motion, then,

9. Review the responses of the plaintiff, determine the need to request more admissions, then report your findings to your attorney. At this point, it may be possible for you to file a Motion for Summary Judgment, if not for a Partial Judgment. At this point in most cases, the case is at-issue.

10. If applicable, and you have not already prepared and filed the same, prepare and file the appropriate document, which in California is called an At-Issue Memorandum, with the court. In most instances, this is a printed form which does not have to be signed by opposing counsel. Just mail a copy to him.

11. After the required statutory time, the court will send out a

document entitled Certificate of Eligibility to File Certificate of Readiness (this document may be under another name in your state). This also is a printed form wherein the court is advising the parties that the case is on the active court list and the parties are now entitled to obtain a trial date.

12. Upon receipt of this document, you can now file what is called in California, a Certificate of Readiness, which is also a printed form, but this document must be signed by both attorneys of record. This document should be calendared so that it can be returned within the required statutory limitation to the court.

13. If for whatever reason, opposing counsel fails to sign and return the Certificate of Readiness (or other such document according to your court rules) in a timely manner, then you should proceed to file a motion and affidavit petitioning the court for a trial date despite the fact that the Certificate of Readiness was not filed in a timely manner.

14. After either one of the above procedures has been accomplished, you will receive from the court a document setting forth the date of trial (and date of settlement conference, if applicable in your state). Upon receipt of this document, you should draft a formal Notice of Trial Date with notification to all parties.

15. Notify all potential witnesses of the trial date.

16. Prepare for trial:
   (a) Review the file and determine what witnesses are to be subpoenaed;
   (b) Prepare the subpoenas and hold them in the file until needed;
   (c) Marshal all trial documents, photos and exhibits, and be sure that they are authenticated;
   (d) Start your trial brief or briefs;
   (e) Draft proposed jury instructions;
   (f) Draft appropriate motions including notice of appeal;
   (g) Draft closing documents and arguments.

## Step-by-Step Procedures

SERVICE ON PERSON OUTSIDE CALIFORNIA BUT WITHIN
UNITED STATES USING LAW OF PLACE WHERE SERVED

HOW ACCOMPLISHED:     In accordance with the law of the place where person served, for this particular type of service.

C.C.P.   §413.10(b)   ([2])

([2])California Codes only.

PROOF OF SERVICE REQUIRED:

That which is required by the law of the place where the person was served.

TIME TO ANSWER:

30 days from date of delivery of the summons and complaint to person served.

DOCUMENTS REQUIRED TO ENTER DEFAULT:

1. Original summons
2. Affidavit setting forth law of place where served (as to particular service)
3. Proof of such service
4. Request for entry of default
5. Proof of mailing request for entry of default

## SERVICE ON PERSON OUTSIDE THE UNITED STATES USING THE FOREIGN LAW

HOW ACCOMPLISHED:

1. As prescribed by the place where the person is served, for this particular type of service.
2. As directed by the foreign authority in response to a letter rogatory.
3. As directed by the court in which the action is pending.

PROOF OF SERVICE REQUIRED:

That which is required by the law of the place where the person was served, or per directions of the court in which the action is pending.

TIME TO ANSWER:

30 days from date of service of the summons and complaint on person served, or in accordance with foreign applicable law if in doubt.

DOCUMENTS REQUIRED TO ENTER DEFAULT:

1. Original summons
2. Affidavit setting forth foreign law as to particular service
3. Proof of such service
4. Request for entry of default
5. Proof of mailing request for entry of default

# Functional Duties During Litigation

*This chapter puts into concrete focus the support activities and duties you can perform and in which you will be involved during the course of assisting your attorney in the practice of his profession.*

# CHAPTER 3

## INTRODUCTION

The purpose of this chapter is to set forth and give an overview of the duties and legal tasks which can safely be performed by you as a legal assistant without infringing upon the practice of law. This, so that you will know what is expected of you as a legal assistant; and, what you can advise your boss about the nature and extent of the duties you can perform to aid him in the practice of his profession.

You should recognize that each law firm, as well as each individual lawyer, may have particular ideas as to how to utilize your special skills. The functional duties set forth in this chapter are merely suggested duties which can be discussed by you and your employer.

### A. Pre-Trial Procedures

1. Interview clients and witnesses.
2. Analyze and draft complaints, cross-complaints, answers, demurrers, motions and accompanying points and authorities and notices.
3. Locate witnesses, records and reports.
4. Serve summons on party litigants and witnesses.
5. Conduct fact-finding from client and outside sources.
6. Prepare case profile with memo to attorney.
7. Draft interrogatories, answers to interrogatories, request for admissions and inspection of documents, questions for depositions and analyze and summarize depositions.

8. Set up a file, including preparation of summaries, digests and indexing of pleadings, law and motion documents, discovery documents, general records and evidence.

9. Organize, summarize and coordinate exhibits for trial.

10. Maintain chronology of the case, including calendaring and scheduling of appearance dates, deposition cases, etc.

11. Prepare pre-trial statements and stipulations.

12. During trial, monitor files, documents and evidence, do spot research, prepare drafts of trial motions, assure presence of witnesses and take notes on testimony of witnesses.

## B. Post-Trial Procedures

13. Prepare notice of appeal.

14. On appeal, analyze documents and testimony for data supporting theories of appeal.

15. Obtain clerk and reporter's transcripts.

16. Draft appellate briefs.

17. After judgment, assist in compliance or enforcement of judgment by locating assets: prepare documentation for collection of judgments and for examination of judgment debtors.

18. Motion for new trial, if applicable.

## THE SUMMARY JUDGMENT

### Introduction

When an answer has been filed, either party can make a motion for summary judgment alleging "no triable issues of fact." If there are no triable issues of fact, only a question of law is left for determination, and questions of law are decided by a judge.

You should know that a motion for summary judgment can be filed as to one cause of action or count. It does not have to be filed against the entire complaint. This situation arises if in your request for admissions you have received an admission that a contract did in fact exist; that the plaintiff did in fact comply with all of the terms of said contract; and the defendant did in fact breach said contract. You can file a summary judgment as to those triable facts and remove them from the trial of the action.

Since sustaining a motion for a summary judgment in favor of your attorney would end the lawsuit, thereby preventing the defendant from having his day in court, it is important that the format and content of said motion be succinctly set forth with utmost clarity. For this reason, consider the following:

I. *In your introduction,* be sure to include the following:

  (a) The complete names and relationships of all parties concerned;

  (b) Spell out separately and distinctly the appearance date and title of the document which made a party-litigant a part of the action;

  (c) Further, as to each party-litigant, the cause or causes of action pertinent; and

  (d) As to each party-litigant, the cause or causes of action said party litigant is not involved in and to which the motion is not directed.

II. *In setting forth the issues:*

  (a) Set forth each and every issue you feel is related and pertinent to the motion for summary judgment;

  (b) As to each of the causes of action involved in your motion for summary judgment, the issue should include:

  (c) The title of the pleading which raised the issue;

  (d) The issue or issues raised in said pleading;

  (e) The name and relationship of the parties against whom the motion is directed.

*Note*: All issues should be separately stated and in numbered paragraphs. And, of course, they should be stated affirmatively.

  (f) Explain, as to each issue, where in the pleading the issue is raised, either by assertive statement or implication; and where it is admitted or denied, either by acquiescence or court rule;

  (g) Set forth the nature and extent of your evidence that proves or disproves the issue being attacked by your motion; and

  (h) How the court is to determine or receive this evidence. (Title of document, with page and line, is sufficient.)

III. *As to your attached declaration,* (client or attorney) it should contain crystal-clear evidence as to each issue raised. The court should be able to discern from this declaration complete and exact reference and/or copies of any and all pertinent evidence.

SAMPLES:

A. Introductions.
    1. Plaintiff _____ moves for summary judgment; or
    2. Plaintiff moves that certain issues be determined to be without controversy; or
    3. Plaintiff _____ moves for summary judgment or in the alternative that certain issues be determined to be without controversy.
    B. This motion for summary judgment is directed against the following individuals and/or corporate entities:
        1. _____ corporation, defendant herein, first appeared on the ____ day of ____, by answering the plaintiff's Complaint on file herein, with respect to First, Third and Seventh Causes of Action. This answering defendant is not involved in any other causes of action.
        2. John Doe, defendant herein, first appeared in the action on the ____ day of ____, by way of demurrer with respect to the Second, Fourth and Eighth Causes of Action of plaintiff's Complaint on file herein. This answering defendant is also involved in the First, Third and Seventh Causes of Action of plaintiff's Complaint against which this motion is directed.

(The above and foregoing are examples of an introduction to a summary judgment.)

## EXAMPLES OF HOW TO LIST YOUR ISSUES

Following is a list of all of the issues pertinent to the within written motion for summary judgment:

"FIRST CAUSE OF ACTION plaintiff alleged in his Complaint and defendant DOE denied as follows:
    1. *Issue:* Plaintiff is a duly licensed general practitioner by way of _____, under License No. ____.
    2. *Pleaded complaint.*
    3. *Defendant DOE answered.*
    4. *Proof:* Certified copy of _____, State License Board, attached hereto as Exhibit A.
    5. *Reference:* Attached declaration of _____, at Page 6, Lines 11 through 18.

\* \* \*

1. *Issue:* Plaintiff and defendant entered into a written contract on the ____ day of ____.

2. *Pleaded:* Complaint, Paragraph 4 defendant DOE answered Paragraph 3.

3. *Admission of Defendant DOE.*

4. *Proof:* Admission of defendant DOE.

5. *Reference:* Attached declaration of _____ at Page 14, Lines 19 and following.''

*Note*: This is a sample of how the issues should be listed, including the four elements of Issue, Pleaded, Proof, and Reference.

## STEP-BY-STEP PROCEDURES

After discussing the file and reviewing the Complaint of plaintiff with your attorney, and it is determined that the case has no merit, or that there is no defense to it, proceed to prepare the following documentation after the time restriction for filing the summary judgment has expired:

1. Notice of Motion and Motion;
2. Declaration of your attorney or client, or both;
3. Memorandum of Points and Authorities in Support of Summary Judgment;
4. If you have had responses to Requests for Admissions, or Answers to Interrogatories; or a deposition, appropriate excerpts or copies of these should be attached or referred to in your Declaration; or in the alternative, request that the court take judicial notice thereof;
5. The above package should be filed and served on opposing counsel at least 10 days prior to the date upon which the motion is set for hearing.

*Caution:* Note that the filing of this motion does not toll or extend the time within which opposing counsel is required to file a responsive pleading. Be sure, therefore, to flag this statutory time period on your file and your ''follow-up'' calendar to avoid a default being taken against your office; or should you want to take a default against opposing counsel.

## Motions with Resulting Orders

Recall the following types of motions:

1. The noticed motion which is normally held in law and motion departments of your Superior Court*;
2. The motion by stipulation which is a mutually agreed upon statement signed by both parties to the action;
3. The ex-parte motion which is normally used in cases of emergency and signed by a Commissioner or Judge;
4. The oral motion which is done in open court;
5. The court's own motion in open court or chambers;
6. The order shortening time.

### EX-PARTE MOTION—EXAMPLE

A client comes into your office on the 30th day and opposing counsel cannot be reached, or if reached, will not grant you an extension of time. What do you do?

You will prepare:
  i. Notice of Motion and Motion for Ex-Parte Order;
 ii. Declaration of your attorney;
iii. Memorandum of Points and Authorities.

Your attorney's declaration should include the following:

1. That the Complaint is long and complex;
2. That he therefore needs the time to fully read it;
3. That he needs the time to verify the facts; or do investigation and research;
4. That he requested the time from opposing counsel and was refused;
5. Set out the points in the Complaint needing verification and research;
6. That he needs the time to accomplish the above in which to prepare an Answer or otherwise plead to the Complaint. (Here within a specific request of time, such as 20 days, 30 days, 60 days, whatever.)

---

*This refers to California practice. The courts of general jurisdiction in other states are often referred to as Circuit Courts, as well as Superior Courts, and in New York State they are referred to as Supreme Courts. However, there may or may not be a law and motion department in other states similar to California practice.

At the very bottom of this package, or on a separate sheet of paper put ORDER.

ORDER

GOOD CAUSE APPEARING, IT IS HEREBY ORDERED that the defendant may have _____ days, up to and including _____ within which to file his Answer or otherwise plead to the plaintiff's Complaint.

Date: _____                    _____

JUDGE

You have an Order to Show Cause hearing pending on a modification. Let us say that the respondent failed to show. Now, instead of a judge letting the case go off calendar, he permits it to be continued for one week.

Say that at the time of the hearing on the Request for Modification, testimony of the petitioner reveals that the respondent failed to perform on an existing Order of the court as to child support and is now in contempt of said prior court Order.

In either of the above, you could prepare an Order to Show Cause re Contempt to be heard on the same date at the same hour as that of the Order to Show Cause re Modification by means of filing a Notice of Motion for An Order Shortening Time.

## Key Practical Procedure

1. Prepare a Notice of Motion and Motion for Order Shortening Time;
2. Prepare a declaration of your attorney;
3. Optional—prepare declaration of client;
4. Prepare Memorandum of Points and Authorities in support thereof;
5. These documents are to be served upon the respondent and his attorney.

## Practical Hint:

Note that your declaration should include a chronological history of the case, the prior orders, need for the order, and why the court should sign same. Importantly, a date certain on which the order can be served should be included therein, bearing in mind the date of the currently scheduled hearing on the modification request.

FOR EXAMPLE:

''Shortening the time within which to serve three (3) days'', or ''Or no later than July ____, 19 ____.''

### Tried and Proven Procedure

We have found it a good practice to prepare a similar supporting affidavit to be signed by the client. So, instead of making it an optional procedure, do it.

### A Must

Be aware that the above package must be served within the time set forth; and that it is a required, mandatory personal service upon the respondent (defendant). Moreover, the signature of the judge must be obtained immediately.

## PROCEDURES FOR FILING MOTIONS
## IN FEDERAL COURT

1. In the Federal Court you have to file the Notice of Motion and Motion at least seventeen (17) days, unless otherwise provided for by the state statute, before the date set for the hearing of the Motion.

2. Opposing counsel thereafter has seven (7) days from the receipt of service of said Motion to file his Memorandum of Law, case authority, and Affidavits in support thereof. Service here is deemed complete upon mailing.

3. You should file the original and one copy (or duplicate originals). *Note* that Federal Courts will now accept Xeroxed copies as long as they are legible. However, you should check with your local Federal Court before proceeding along these lines.

4. On the motions for the production of documents, if the list is too long; or, if there is controversy as to the need for certain documents in question, the court will send out an Order requiring the parties to meet and decide on one mutual document.

The parties thereafter have two (2) weeks to perform or reply to this request. Your job in this regard is to review the documents with your attorney and draft a Joint Statement with opposing counsel or his legal assistant.

## Reminder:

Recall the following Preliminary Motions which can be filed:

1. *A Motion For A More Definite Statement.* Remember, this Motion is similar to the State Court's Special Demurrer.

2. *A Motion to Strike.* This, too, is the same as the State Court's Motion, except that in the Federal Court you can bring an Interlocutory Appeal if the Motion to Strike is granted.

3. *A Motion for Judgment on the Pleadings.* This is similar to the General Demurrer in the State Court system where only the pleadings are considered. You should also remember that under Rule 12(c) of the Federal Rules of Civil Procedure this Motion may be made after the pleadings are closed, but only at a time that will not delay the trial of the action.

4. *A Motion for Summary Judgment.* Remember that under Rule 56 of the Federal Rules of Civil Procedure, the parties making and opposing a Motion for Summary Judgment are permitted to file Affidavits in support of their requested arguments. And finally,

5. *Motion for Partial Summary Judgment Under Rule 56 (c) for Liability Alone.*

## THE INJUNCTIVE PROCESS

The following injunctive process may be initiated and may occur prior to the actual trial of a case, with a full hearing on the merits of the claim.

1. Prepare your Complaint in which you incorporate your request for a Temporary Restraining Order;

2. Prepare a Memorandum of Points and Authorities In Support Thereof;

3. Prepare a Declaration or Affidavit for your attorney, or if preferred, one for your client. You should also attach to your Affidavit or Declaration an Order to Show Cause;

4. Prepare your Ex Parte Notice and Motion, since this is an ex parte procedure.

*Note*: Do not forget to attach your Order for the convenience of the judge and be aware of your statutory time limitations for service on the defendant.

5. Be sure to serve the defendant, personally, with all pleadings heretofore filed with the court regarding the case at bar.

If successful, the results of the hearing will be the issuance of a Preliminary Injunction which would be in force and effect until the trial of the matter. At the trial, a Permanent Injunction may issue.

## PREPARING YOUR BRIEF

The timing in filing a brief is part of the strategy used by your attorney in prosecuting a lawsuit. At any point during the course of a triable action, he may ask you to prepare a brief just on the issues of liability, for example, to be presented to the court the next morning. This sudden move on his part might catch opposing counsel off-guard since he would not be expecting such an event.

To prepare this brief, you would look to the issues raised in the Complaint and the affirmative defenses set forth in the Answer to the Complaint. Thereafter, it is a matter of legal research to find supporting case authority for each issue.

### Personal Observation

Being a good brief writer does not mean that you have superior writing skills, or even any writing skill. Brief writing is a skill that can be learned and improved upon with practice, more practice, and even more practice. We have found that a legal assistant must present a ''lawyer-like'' approach in preparing trial briefs to be used by the attorney. This preparation will require you to think and argue as an attorney would. If you adopt this approach, much time and effort will be saved by your attorney in revising the trial brief.

With this in mind, you, as the legal assistant preparing the trial brief, must be mindful that your brief will be read by a judge with a ''knowing eye'' and that he is the person you must persuade as to the issues raised and the points and authorities submitted in support thereof. By looking at the trial brief from the standpoint of a disinterested observer, you are able to evaluate your own work critically and ensure that the trial brief makes common sense as well as legal sense.

## Self-Analysis

In order to be successful in preparing a trial brief, you must be able to stand back and make an objective analysis of the product. Be able to recognize your mistakes and weaknesses—and laugh at them—then proceed to correct the mistakes and strengthen the weaknesses.

Being able to recognize these factors and to correct them is the first step toward improvement and good writing skills. Don't ever be afraid of a mistake, for it is the only vehicle for self-improvement. And self-criticism will enable you to accept criticism from your attorney.

Though the trip through the maze to find the correct words and phrases may be frustrating at times for the novice litigation legal assistant, there are some fundamental steps which can assist you in expanding your writing skills and developing the proper approach.

1. *Is the trial brief a trial brief?*

You want to be concise and to the point in wording the trial brief, much like your memorandum of law as heretofore discussed. This is because judges have heavy case loads and, of necessity, must review trial briefs in a cursory manner. Therefore, it is important that you get to the point of your brief as quickly as possible. A long, complicated dissertation on the complexities of the law applicable is undesirable—and I kid you not, is rarely read by a busy judge.

2. *Does it flow?*

It is important that you use effective, transitional sentences. A brief cannot be molded into an effective argument if unrelated paragraphs are thrown together. Each paragraph must pick up the significance of the last paragraph or section and entice the reader to continue to read.

3. *Have you anticipated the positive and eliminated the negative?*

The trial brief must always highlight the strong points of your argument. Bearing in mind the cursory manner in which judges read trial briefs, always try to state at the very beginning the point and leading case authority on which you feel the judge will most likely agree. Remember, judges know the law and the leading cases, as well as you do. This approach will put the judge in a good psychological position for any points or authorities that will follow with which he may not agree. Do not freeze because you feel you may not know the leading cases;—or, get overconfi- dent because you feel you do. Your attorney will tell you the strongest points in the cases he wants and will know the leading cases in the field which are applicable.

4. *Are the cases unfavorable to your argument, adequately dis- posed of?*

NEVER, NEVER underestimate the adversary.

You must anticipate any significant cases which oppose your position. Do not be surprised by the opposition placing great emphasis on cases which you feel are not in point. The only sure method to remove the force of opposing cases is to distinguish them from the facts of your case. How do you do that?

It takes time to develop the skill. It requires close reading of the facts of the unfavorable cases and the reasoning of the courts behind their decisions. If the courts strongly emphasize the facts as the basis for their decisions, you have a good opportunity to dispose of unfavorable decisions merely on the statement of a factual situation—that is, of course, if they are markedly different.

5. *Does the brief impress or persuade?*

Please, do not become a ''bluff techniquer''—meaning the listing of long streams of citations and extensive footnotes. Always remember that the judge could care less and does not have the time to read them anyway. Moreover, too many footnotes will destroy the continuity of your argument by interrupting its flow. Use them sparingly. Do not take the mind of the judge away from the main point by having him evaluate issues collateral to your main argument.

The use of streams of citations has even a greater potential to danger—it may have the effect of damaging your argument. Not only does it interrupt the continuity of your brief, but it may raise a suspicion in the mind of the judge as to whether or not they are on point. It would be better to cite a recent case in which all of the cases referred to are incorporated. Or, you might want to give time to an article or form book that mentions and explains the earlier cases.

## Practical Hint

To aid you in developing your brief-writing skills, it is suggested that you compile a diversified form of trial briefs, i.e., full-blown, or one-issue trial briefs, legal memoranda, etc. At every opportunity you should take the time to read and examine closely trial briefs and study the format and style. Attempting to evaluate successful trial briefs will most certainly improve and enhance your brief-writing ability.

## PREPARING YOUR EXHIBITS

### Helpful Hint:

It has been our experience that an exhibit folder should be immediately made up and applicable documents labeled, indexed and placed therein. You should do this when and as exhibits come into your office. This will enable your attorney to find a document quickly and easily at any given moment in the prosecution of the case.

Consider the following steps:

1. Maintain the original of any particular exhibit in the exhibit folder with a copy to the:

    (a) Evidence file;

    (b) Chronological file folders.

2. Each document (or other type of exhibit) should be dated;

3. Note the source of exhibit by either staple or clip to the copy, but never, and I repeat, never, staple the original document.

4. Divide into categories, such as purchase orders, contracts, tax returns, medical reports, and so forth.

*Note*: All medical reports should be divided into plaintiff's medical reports and defendant's medical reports.)

Together with the exhibit file, you should prepare these additional folders:

1. Pleading folder which contains:

    (a) Plaintiff's motion papers and a separate division for defendant's motion papers;

    (b) Summary of the allegations of the Complaint;

    (c) Summary of the Answer and Affirmative Defenses;

    (d) Summary of your attorney's defenses;

    (e) Summary of issues left to be tried; and

    (f) Summary of facts to be included at the time of trial.

2. Trial brief, if applicable (full-blown or issue).

3. List all the information about the jury panel, including, but not

limited to, their names, addresses, telephone numbers, occupation, political allegiance, hobbies, etc.

    4. A witness folder containing:

    (a) Separate statements about each individual witness;

    (b) Any notes taken at an interview of a witness;

    (c) Any investigation reports;

    (d) Summary of any deposition; or

    (e) Statements made by witness.

    5. Document folder which contains the documents to be presented into evidence; this should be tagged and placed in chronological order according to subject matter.

    6. A legal research folder containing:

    (a) Law memoranda in support of your attorney's position;

    (b) Law memoranda in support of opposing counsel's petition; and

    (c) Law memoranda in rebuttal.

    7. Motion folder containing any possible motion the attorney may wish to bring during the course of a trial, such as, Motion for Summary Judgment, Motion for Mistrial, Motion for Dismissal, and the like.

    8. A folder containing potential and possible jury instructions; and

    9. A folder containing notes for your attorney's final argument.

    10. The Exhibit Book. This book is prepared when the trial is completed, but before counsels for the party litigants give their final arguments to the jury, or judge sitting without a jury. It should contain exhibits submitted by each party litigant, including those used for identification purposes. This book is a must.

### Introduction to Forms

    The following sample Summary Judgment and Motion for Summary Judgment forms are provided for illustrative purposes. Be aware that these forms are used only when you are sure that you can win the case by filing such a motion. Note that the filing of this motion does not toll or extend the time within which opposing counsel is required to file a responsive pleading. For this reason, be sure to flag the statute of limitations on your file and your follow-up or "come-up" calendar to avoid a default being taken against your attorney; or should you want to take a default, against the opposing counsel.

## MOTION FOR SUMMARY JUDGMENT

Attorneys for Plaintiff.

SUPERIOR COURT OF THE STATE OF _____
FOR THE COUNTY OF _____

|  |  |  |
|---|---|---|
| Plaintiff, | ) | No. |
| | ) | |
| vs. | ) | (NOTICE FOR) MOTION |
| | ) | FOR SUMMARY JUDGMENT |
| | ) | FOR PLAINTIFF: |
| | ) | DECLARATION AND POINTS |
| | ) | AND AUTHORITIES IN SUPPORT |
| | ) | THEREOF. |
| | ) | |
| | ) | Hearing Date:   May 30, 19__ |
| _____  Defendants. | ) | |
| | | Department 18, 9:30 a.m. |

TO DEFENDANTS, AND EACH OF THEM, AND TO THEIR RESPEC-TIVE ATTORNEYS OF RECORD:

NOTICE is hereby given that on May 30, 19__, at 9:30 a.m. or as soon thereafter as the matter may be heard in the courtroom of Department 18, of the above entitled court located at _____, _____, the plaintiff, _____ will move the court for an order striking the answers of defendants _____, and _____ and for entry of summary judgment in favor of plaintiff against said defendants as prayed in the complaint on file herein.

Said motion will be made on the ground that there is no defense on the action on the bond.

Said motion will be based upon this notice, the pleadings, records, the files herein, upon the declaration and memorandum of Points and Authorities served and filed in support of this motion for summary judgment.

Dated _____

_____

SUMMARY JUDGMENT

Attorney for Plaintiff

_____
_____

NO.

_____,

     Plaintiff, )   SUMMARY JUDGMENT
         )   pursuant to Section
         )   of the Code of Civil
  vs.       )   Procedure
         )
_____, )
     Defendant. )

   This cause having come on regularly to be heard in Department ____ of the above entitled Court, the Honorable _____, Judge presiding, on August 6, 19__, pursuant to duly noticed motion for summary judgment. _____ appearing for the moving party; and _____ appearing for the responding party; and the Court having considered the pleadings, the documents presented and filed with respect to the motion and particularly the affidavits or declarations, and having heard and considered the contentions of counsel; and the Court having heretofore granted the said motion on the statutory ground that there is no defense to the action and that no triable issue of fact is presented:

   IT IS ORDERED that the answer of defendant, _____, be, and it is, stricken;

   IT IS FURTHER ADJUDGED AND DECREED that plaintiff, _____ _____, have judgment against the defendant, _____, in the sum of _____ as principal, and the sum of _____ as interest, and the sum of _____ as and for attorney's fees, for a total sum of _____, together with costs in the sum of _____.

   Dated this _____ day of _____, 19__.

_____
     JUDGE OF SUPERIOR COURT

# Guidelines for Preparing a Legal Memorandum

# CHAPTER 4

*Since one of the most important duties you will ever have in a law office is legal research, this skill is potentially one of the greatest time-savers in any law office.*

## INTRODUCTION

You will recall that the purpose of writing a legal memorandum is to inform your attorney and other members of the firm and to give a current status of the law (in which you set forth both sides of the question), making a recommendation, if possible—and if not, being sure to state that you have no recommendation; and if the law is clear on the issue raised, making a conclusion.

You should allow at least 3 or 4 hours for the preparation and completion of such a legal memorandum, unless the problem is filled with complexities. Then, several days of concentrated, uninterrupted research would be proper.

Despite the fact that you may have just completed a paralegal course, do not be afraid to ask questions concerning the content and purpose of the legal memorandum when being instructed by your attorney. Most attorneys prefer that you ask the questions prior to commencement of a job, rather than during the performance, and certainly, not after completion. To do otherwise, causes irritation. To follow the aforementioned shows alertness and humility.

As an aid to taking notes, it is suggested that you develop abbreviations of words most often used by your attorney. This will be of extreme value in discussing the assignment and later reading and making notes for the cases found. For example:

Plaintiff = plts.
Triangle mark for defendant.
BFP = bona fide purchaser.
c/p = community property.
x = comp-cross-complaint or cross-complainant
PI = personal injury.
Comp. case = Workmen's Compensation.
S/L = statute of limitation.
S/F = statute of frauds.

## STEP-BY-STEP PROCEDURES

In drafting the legal memorandum, consider the following:

1. Develop an approach by using an outline or chart. This will enable you to clearly understand not only what it is your attorney wants, but it will help you determine what methods you should use to get the desired results.

2. Pick out the phrase or theory that clearly sets forth the proposition or issues you want to support. Then, commence reading the cases which come closest to the issue or issues involved—and of course, those that are in opposition to the problem proposed.

3. When attacking the legal research project, your point of reference is the applicable state code, i.e., Penal Code, Civil Code, Probate Code, etc. These sources, as a general rule, will usually point you in the right direction. In proceeding with your research, it is fatal to overlook or forget to check the supplements to the codes (pocket parts, as they are commonly called); or the advance sheets published by the Appellate Court system.

4. As you read, make notes on 3x5 cards or a legal tablet designed especially for that purpose, noting the key points raised which lean toward the issues of your case. For easy referral, always note the book, volume, page number, paragraph and section of each case read and to be re-read.

5. The easiest way to do this is to look at the heading of each case on the "front or fact sheet" of the case (sometimes called the "Table of Contents"). These two sections of a case will tell you if the case is for or

against your proposition, and if so, to what extent, alleviating the necessity of your having to read the case in its entirety.

6. Should the case be on target, SHEPARDIZE it again. Failure to do so may cause your attorney to walk into court and get mud on his face if the case has been overruled or superseded by another more recent decision.

Your legal memorandum should include the following:

1. Statement of Facts
2. Issue or Issues
3. Discussion
4. Answer, and
5. Conclusion

A. In citing a case, always place the official report first, but also give the unofficial report citation. For example, in California we would cite a case as follows: *People v. Gould* (1971), 54 CA 2d 621; 7 Cal. Rptr. 273; 354 P.2d 30. Cal., being the official reports, and the unofficial reports being California Reporter (Cal. Rptr.) and the Pacific Reporter (P.) which includes 9 other states outside California.

B. When copying the statutes if you find that certain portions of the statute are underlined in the Code book, do not underline them when you quote the statute. The lines under the words are not part of the statute. They merely tell the reader that those words are new to the statute. This applies also to the asterisk which may be found in the text of a statute being quoted in a code.

C. In setting off quotations, citations, etc., indent on both paragraphs for a single space. Do not use quotation marks when indenting.

D. In citing old cases, say so and explain the connection and your purpose for including them in your memorandum.

## Pitfalls

E. One of the greatest pitfalls in citing cases is the use of the words, "supra," "infra," and "ibid." Know them, their meanings, and use them properly.

*Supra* (always underline), means—that which came before;

*Infra* (always underline), means—that which comes later;

*Ibid* (always underline), means—on the same page or in the same book.

F. In your discussions use strong phrases such as, ''The bulk of case authority states that..'' or, ''The law is clear..'', and so forth.

G. Be relevant; never forget the case you are discussing. Always tie in your case law and authority with the subject matter of your legal memorandum. In other words, do not lose sight of your objectives and ramble.

H. In your conclusion, list or refer, or even incorporate your leading citations, and lastly,

I. Make it readable, interesting, but more important, brief.

Thereafter, of course, you should sit down with your attorney and discuss what you have done, remembering always that he is the final authority.

## SHEPARDIZING

### Introduction

One of the most important duties of a legal assistant is that of legal research. This function, skillfully used, is potentially one of the greatest timesavers in any law office. It is considered by some to be the most meaningful and significant of the legal tasks performed by legal assistants. The purpose of this section is to introduce you to the basic steps in a research situation and show you how to use that knowledge in drafting a legal memorandum for the benefit of your attorney.

Simply put, the art of Shepardizing is merely the way you confirm or disaffirm the law as it stands at the point in time you wish to use it—and how it got there. And further, that the point of law your attorney is planning to use has not been vacated or superseded (or other like ruling) by a decision reached in the appellate courts.

In the legal arena what happens in the trial courts has little effect on the evolution of law. It is the appellate courts which tell you how the lower courts and legal researchers will write the law. With this process in mind, scholars and students of the law came up with the tools of research to aid the legal profession to quickly and accurately find the latest decisions or interpretations of the law as created by the courts. One such legal tool is referred to as Shepardizing. To aid you in determining the status of a case, Shepard's citations have broken down the procedure as follows:

The history of a case, which reflects what happened to a case on appeal, denoted as follows:

| | |
|---|---|
| a - | affirmed |
| cc - | connected case |
| D - | dismissed |
| M - | modified |
| r - | reversed |
| s - | same case |
| S - | superseded |
| v - | vacated |
| US - | cert den |
| US - | cert dis |
| US - | reh den |
| US - | reh dis |

The phrase "Treatment of a Case" refers to the decisions reached by the judiciary and is denoted as follows:

| | |
|---|---|
| c - | criticized |
| d - | distinguished |
| e - | explained |
| f - | followed |
| h - | harmonized |
| k - | dissenting opinion |
| L - | limited |
| O - | overruled |
| p - | parallel |
| q - | question |
| v - | vacated |

## Step-by-Step Procedure for Shepardizing

1. Check the applicable code, statute or other source. The result of this procedure will give you a case or cases on point with the issue or issues raised in your problem.

2. This being true, you are now ready to Shepardize.

3. If, after reading the headnote and complete case you feel that it is on target with your problem, you would then go to the Shepard's volume (checking the applicable supplement) containing the report in which the case appears.

4. There could conceivably be a column of 20 to 30 treatment items under this case, which would require further Shepardizing on your part.

5. You would, therefore, have to look to each reference where the case was so cited to determine if the decision reached therein was either overturned, sustained, superseded, etc.

6. You would follow the above Shepardizing procedure for each and every reference cited and until you are satisfied that:

    (a)  The case was on point;

    (b)  The case was not on point; or

    (c)  That the decision has been overruled or affirmed by subsequent decisions.

Consider the following boilerplate forms for developing a memorandum of points and authorities in support of whatever motion you are preparing for filing. Note that the first one is for a partial summary judgment and is a "full-blown" memorandum in that it sets out the procedural facts, the preliminary facts, the argument and the conclusion; as opposed to the second memorandum in support of a demurrer, which is short and merely states what the State Code of Civil Procedure requires to substantiate a cause of action. Depending on what your attorney requires, you can use either of these forms and be safe.

*Practical Hint:* Remember that a copy of this memorandum should be accompanied by a declaration when mailing the same to opposing counsel and filing the original with the court.

## MEMORANDUM OF POINTS AND AUTHORITIES IN SUPPORT OF MOTION FOR PARTIAL SUMMARY JUDGMENT

Plaintiff, in support of the motion for partial summary judgment, submits the following:

### PROCEDURAL FACTS

A Motion for Partial Summary Judgment was filed by plaintiff in the _____ Superior Court on August 7, 19__. The court took no action on said motion because defendants petitioned for removal of the case to the United States District Court.

That plaintiff made a motion to remove the case to the Los Angeles Superior Court, and said motion having been granted and the case remanded to the _____ Superior Court, plaintiff now seeks to renew her motion for Partial Summary Judgment.

### PRELIMINARY FACTS

Plaintiff used the services of defendant _____ _____, a second mortgage loan broker, to borrow money to pay her real property taxes (See Broker's Loan Statement and Disclosure Statement, attached hereto as Exhibit 1 and Exhibit 2, respectively). In connection with the loan, plaintiff was required to sign, in addition to a note and second trust deed, an Agency and Servicing Agreement, attached hereto as Exhibit 3, which required her *to make monthly payments thirty (30) days in advance of the due date on the* (emphasis added); plaintiff was approximately four (4) days late under the terms of the Agency and Servicing Agreement and was assessed and paid a late charge in the amount of Eighteen ($18.00) Dollars.

### ARGUMENT

The Late Charges assessed under the Agency and Servicing Agreement do not qualify as liquidated damages and are therefore void under *Civil Code,* Section 1670.

*Civil Code,* Section 1670, provides:

"Every contract by which the amount of damage to be paid, or other compensation to be made, for a breach of an obligation, is determined in anticipation thereof, is to that extent void, except as expressly provided in the next section."

Section 1671 defines and authorizes a liquidation of damages stating ....

## MEMORANDUM OF POINTS AND AUTHORITIES IN SUPPORT OF DEMURRER

### I

*California Code of Civil Procedure, Section 430.1(f) authorizes a demurrer on the ground that the pleading does not state facts sufficient to constitute a cause of action.*
*Code of Civil Procedure,* Section 430.10, provides in part as follows:

"The party against whom a complaint ... has been filed may object, by demurrer ... as provided in Section 430.30, to the pleading on any one or more of the following grounds:

....

(f) The pleading does not state facts sufficient to constitute a cause of action."

### CONCLUSION

Defendants do not seek the sustaining of their Demurrer without leave to amend, but only to be served with a proper complaint which complies with the laws of the State of _____. For these reasons, the court should exercise its discretion to sustain defendants' demurrer, and require the case to go forward, if at all, on the foundation of a proper complaint.

Dated: _____    _____

### OR

WHEREFORE, these demurring defendants pray that this Demurrer be sustained without leave to amend; that plaintiffs take nothing by way of their complaint; that the action be dismissed and defendants have judgment for their costs and such other relief as the court may deem just and proper.

Dated: _____    _____

# Functional Duties of a Legal Assistant in the Discovery Process

# CHAPTER 5

*Knowing when and how to use the vehicle of discovery is what winning a case is all about. In this chapter you are reminded how to develop the necessary discovery documents so important to the successful conclusion of your attorney's case.*

## INTRODUCTION

In most state court systems, as well as in the federal court system, the nature and extent of allowable discovery are governed by statute. The federal rules relating to discovery are found in the Federal Rules of Civil Procedure. These Federal Rules of Civil Procedure are not binding on the state court systems' discovery procedures, but merely serve as a guide.

Rule 33 of the Federal Rules of Civil Procedure brought about major changes and differences between state and federal practice. As a consequence, you, as a legal assistant, should be aware of the dissimilarity between the federal and state procedures relating to pleadings and the rules testing those pleadings, since the scope of discoverable material may be quite different.

FOR YOUR REVIEW, RECALL THE FIVE "WHY'S" OF DISCOVERY:

1. To obtain the additional information at the least expense to the client;
2. To negate and avoid the "surprise" evidence or witness at the time of trial, and to share the results of any investigation;
3. To reduce triable issues, thereby shortening the duration of a trial;
4. To preserve evidence for testimony of witnesses;
5. To give a preview of opposing counsel's case.

## What Is Discovery:

### ABBREVIATED DEFINITIONS

1. Interrogatories—written questions
2. Depositions—mini-trial situations
3. Production of Documents—motion
4. Physical and Psychological Exams—motion
5. Request for Admissions—written statements, and
6. Request for Production of Stationary Objects—motion

There is no reason why your attorney should go into court to try a lawsuit without knowing everything there is to know about the opposition's case. Discovery is the tool by which he can do this, and at the same time, prepare his case for trial.

This is the area in a law practice where your services as a legal assistant, and your special skills, can be used efficiently. Consider the following reasons:

1. An attorney should not be required or expected to spend his valuable time helping a client answer interrogatories or in the marshalling of interrogatories.

2. He should not have to spend countless hours reviewing a complaint or answer with a client's file in preparation for preparing a responsive pleading thereof; or in preparation to marshal a set of Requests for Admissions or in answering such Requests.

3. Nor should your attorney be required or expected to review complaints, interrogatories, documents and other exhibits to see that they are authenticated; that all necessary documents are present in the file BEFORE going to court; or to determine the feasibility or timeliness of preparing a Motion to Produce; a Bill of Particulars; a Statement of Damages or a Motion for Summary Judgment;

4. Nor should he have to determine from the file and documents therein what witnesses, if any, should be deposed; or if in fact have been deposed, and so on. These are the time-consuming legal tasks which are your bailiwick. In recapitulating your duties in the area of the discovery process, consider the following:

# I. PLAINTIFF'S PROCEDURE IN THE DISCOVERY PROCESS

Developing interrogatories is a matter of deductive reasoning. You must first determine what it is you are attempting to accomplish and what you are seeking to obtain from the questions, or statements, if it is a Request for Admissions. Just ask yourself, ''Will these questions (or statements) obtain the desired results?'' If your answer is yes, then you are on the right track.

## A. Interrogatories.

STEP-BY-STEP PROCEDURE

1. Develop your interrogatories based upon what information your attorney is seeking to obtain.

2. The first thing you do is look to the Complaint to determine the contentions of the client, and the alleged wrongs committed by the defendant. Then look to the Answer for any affirmative defenses of the defendant;

3. Once these facts are thoroughly imprinted in your mind, you are ready to develop your interrogatories or request for admissions.

4. The first several interrogatories will be directed to personal data, i.e., name, address, telephone number, occupation or business, and so forth;

5. It is suggested that you have the contentions of the defendant in front of you on a tablet as it makes for easier referral in following your thoughts while developing your interrogatories.

EXAMPLE:

CONTENTION NO. 1: That plaintiff has, on several occasions demanded of defendant, the return of his deposit and the defendant has failed and refused to return said deposit.

INTERROGATORY NO. 1: Between the dates January 1, 19__ and June, 19__, did you receive any correspondence from the plaintiff regarding the subject matter of the within complaint?

INTERROGATORY NO. 2: If the answer to Interrogatory No. 1 is yes, please list the date or dates of said correspondence, and state your willingness to have the same produced for inspection and/or copying.

6. Once they have been developed and mailed to the defendant, calendar for the return of the answers.

7. When the answers are received, review them very carefully since from these answers, you will be developing your requests for admissions or setting a deposition of a witness; or your attorney may wish to copy or inspect documents referred to therein.

## B. Request for Admissions

It is upon the same theory of deductive reasoning that you develop your request for admissions. Only in this instance, you would be attempting to secure admissions as to the truth of the statement of fact in order to remove triable issues of fact.

1. In developing your request for admissions, determine what it is your attorney wants admitted or accomplished by this discovery vehicle, then review the complaint, the answer to the complaint, and answers to the interrogatories (if applicable). Thereafter, analytically develop your request to accomplish this purpose.

FOR EXAMPLE:

REQUEST FOR ADMISSION NO. 1: Admit that you entered into a contract with the plaintiff on January 27, 19__, for the purchase of the subject real property.

REQUEST FOR ADMISSION NO. 2: Admit that you gave to plaintiff as a deposit, in good faith, toward the purchase of said real property, the sum of $5,000.00.

REQUEST FOR ADMISSION NO. 3: Admit that you signed the necessary preliminary documents, as required by law, to approve your application for a loan covering the balance of the purchase price of said real property.

REQUEST FOR ADMISSION NO. 4: Admit that your first demand for the return of your deposit was made on or about July 1, __.

And so on.

2. Then calendar the request for admissions on the day you mail them out for return within the statutory period. This return date should be noted on your desk calendar, office master calendar and also on the file folder, as well as the memo to the file.

## II. DEFENDANT'S PROCEDURE IN THE DISCOVERY PROCESS

### A. Interrogatories

1. If your office is the recipient of interrogatories, note the date of receipt of said interrogatories on the appropriate statute book, file folder or memo to file sheet, if used.

2. Xerox a copy of the questions and mail them to the client with a covering letter for review and answer with instructions to return the same within a specified time period. Experience has taught us that a copy should be mailed, together with tablet paper, for the convenience of the client in writing out the answers. Further, it has been proven that a letter of explanation as to what they are and why they are needed is expedient. You should include in your letter the statutory limitation period for the return of the answers and request that the client call should he need help in reducing the answers to writing.

3. As an alternative, set up an appointment for the client to come into the office so that you may work with him in aiding him to answer the questions to the best of his knowledge.

4. Upon receipt of a set of interrogatories, note the date of receipt of said interrogatories on the appropriate statute book, file folder or memo to the file sheet, if used.

5. Xerox a copy of the questions and mail them to the client with a covering letter for review and answer, with instructions to return the answers within a specified time. Then note the return date on the file and your desk calendar. Alternatively, set up an appointment for the client to come into the office so that you may work with him in answering the questions to the best of his knowledge.

(Experience has taught us that a copy should be mailed together with tablet paper for the convenience of the client in writing out the answers. Further, it has been proven that a letter of explanation as to what they are and why they are needed, is expedient.)

6. ALWAYS, without exception, should the client not return the answers within the time prescribed, as set forth in your letter, a request for extension should be immediately secured from opposing counsel and confirmed via letter. (It is at this point that you (may) would make any

objections to the interrogatories as propounded, and file the appropriate document pertinent, i.e. "Objections to Interrogatories." This, of course, would be according to office policy or your attorney's choice.)

7. In any event, when the answers are received, compare them to the attorney's notes in the file, the interview and in-take sheet, and any other documentation in the file, to be sure they are correct to the best of the client's knowledge and belief.

## B. Request for Admissions

1. As the recipient of requests for admissions, since the answers to the statements can determine the liability or non-liability of the client thereby affecting the outcome of a lawsuit, you should be guided by your attorney in preparing the answers.

2. Obtaining the answers to a request for admissions, as a general rule, should be handled in the same manner as with the answers to interrogatories as hereinabove set forth. You are cautioned, however, to carefully review the contents of the file, i.e., your in-take sheet, complaint allegations, the answer to the complaint, and the answers to the interrogatories, if applicable.

3. Once the answers have been prepared, and approved by your attorney, obtain the client's signature in the same way as with the answers to interrogatories set forth above.

## DEPOSITION—PROCEDURE AS TO BOTH LITIGANTS

From the answers to interrogatories and/or request for admissions, your attorney will have determined if he wants to depose a witness or a party to the action; or if there is a need for production and copying or inspection of documents. Your functional duties in this regard are set forth hereinafter.

1. You can explain the nature of a deposition, what it is, i.e., a mini-trial with a court reporter, defense attorney and his own attorney present.

2. You can review the facts of the case, i.e., refresh the client's memory as to the date, time and place of the accident; how it occurred (NOT WHO WAS AT FAULT), i.e., the speed at which the client was driving; where they were going; whether or not it was work-related, and the like.

3. If the client was injured as a result of an automobile accident, then you can review or permit the client to review the medical reports prepared and submitted by the doctors involved. You, as a Legal Assistant, cannot explain the meaning of what the doctor states in his report; or attempt to rationalize differences in the reports of the doctors. *This is the Attorney's bailiwick and what the Attorney must and should do.*

4. If needed, and asked to, or as a vehicle of experience, you can sit in on a deposition as long as the attorney of record is present.

5. If it is merely a question of copying and reproducing documents brought to a deposition as a result of a notice to produce or *subpoena duces tecum,* you may sit in on a deposition and only under these circumstances, unless otherwise instructed and/or permitted by the attorney.

In summary, however, either party can set a deposition by way of the following:

1. Oral agreement;
2. Stipulation; or
3. On notice.

A non-party deposition must be subpoenaed first, before the deposition in fact can be held.

If the party resides out of the state, the deposition must be held within 75 miles; and if it is held outside of the area, then the moving party must go to the witness; or in the alternative, secure letters rogatory or commission (please check your local code and court rules to see whether this procedure is applicable.) In California, these are orders of a California court requesting a court in another state to issue its subpoena directing the attendance of one of its citizens at a deposition.

## DISCOVERY—DIGESTING THE DEPOSITION

### Purpose

The digest is used as a tool by attorneys at the trial of a lawsuit for the following reasons:

1. To condense testimony by making it more manageable;
2. To verify the facts in a case, such as, how fast the defendant was driving, how many drinks defendant had, etc.;
3. To provide your attorney with a quick index of testimony;
4. To aid the attorney's direct and cross-examination of a witness during trial;

5. To aid the attorney to quickly detect inconsistencies in testimony; and

6. To lay the foundation for a motion to produce during the discovery process.

## Checklist in Comparing a Deposition Summary

1. Listen carefully to instructions from your attorney and take notes of the points he wants verified;
2. Determine the foregoing in specifics and establish why it is important;
3. Check to see if there is a possible violation of state statutes;
4. Read at least 4 to 5 pages ahead of yourself to allow the testimony to fall into place, and/or make sense to you. Do not dive head-on into reading, attempting to digest it all at once—this is fatal!
5. As the first few pages are normally preliminary statements for identification, you can pass over them quickly, and you should;
6. If applicable, draw a schematic map, diagram or chart to explain what you have done; and
7. Ignore the "objections" in the deposition as spoken by the defendant's attorney;
8. Once you begin, read through the entire deposition in a cursory way, attempting to spot testimony relative to your attorney's issues;
9. Note the questions regarding issues immediately before the answer, and the answer given to the question;
10. After the foregoing has been accomplished to your satisfaction,—
11. Re-read the deposition slowly and carefully to get the overall context of the matter clearly in your mind, paying particular attention to the conversations before and after each issue raised;
12. Once again, make brief notations of your findings relating to the inconsistencies, including line and page;
13. If possible (or applicable), read the deposition of another material witness for comparison, noting the page and line of any statement made relative to the points at issue; and
14. Prepare your summary (brief), attach it to the applicable deposition, and give it to your attorney. (*Note:* Keep it brief. You are supposed to be saving him time.)

## ENFORCEMENT ORDERS (SANCTIONS)
## (As to Depositions and Interrogatories)

### A. Depositions

Recall the basis upon which you can apply for a motion to compel further answers or for sanctions as follows:

1) You can request the court to strike all or portions of any pleadings heretofore filed by the defendant;
2) You can request the court to dismiss the complaint, or portions thereof;
3) You can request the court to enter a judgment by default against the defendant and in favor of plaintiff;
4) You can request the court to limit the proof which opposing counsel may present at the time of trial; and
5) You can request such other and further relief as the court deems just and proper, including but not limited to attorney fees.

### B. Interrogatories

KEY PROCEDURES:
1) You can compel election of expert or lay witnesses; or
2) You can compel further answers to interrogatories.

To determine when to compel, remember that the following elements should be present:

1) That the answers are inadequate;
2) That the answers are not responsive;
3) That the answers are incomplete.

If either or all of the above are present, then prepare a Motion to Compel Further Answers, which motion should be accompanied by a declaration of your attorney including the following:

1) The areas in which the answers are inadequate;
2) The areas in which the answers are incomplete;
3) The areas in which the answers are not responsive.

*Note*: With reference to items 1, 2, and 3 above, be sure to include the number of the interrogatory as well as the page and line at which it is found, as well as the interrogatory itself.

4) Then request the court to impose sanctions for failure of the defendant to comply.

## C. Summary of Functional Duties of a Paraprofessional in the Area of Interrogatories, Request for Admissions and Depositions

After service has been accomplished, that is service of Summons and Complaint, immediately determine when your attorney wishes to start his discovery, then proceed as follows:

A) *Plaintiff*—With reference to the interrogatories:

1) Develop your interrogatories based upon what information your attorney is seeking.

2) Once they have been developed and mailed to defendant, calendar for the return of the answers.

3) Upon receipt of the answers, review them carefully, since from them you will be developing your Request for Admissions; or setting a deposition of a witness or the defendant; or determining whether or not there are documents which the attorney may wish to inspect and copy.

B) *Defendant*—

1) On the other side of the coin, if you are the recipient of interrogatories, immediately mail them out to the client.

*Cautionary Measure:* Experience has taught us that a copy should be mailed, together with a sheet of tablet paper for the client to write his answers. Also, write a letter of explanation as to what the interrogatories are and why they are needed, and specifically set forth the time limitation for the return of the answers; or have the client call for help in reducing the answers to writing.

2) If the client needs help, set up an office appointment for him to come in.

3) After the foregoing has been accomplished, compare the answers with the attorney notes in the file, the interview sheet, the in-take sheet, and/or any other documentation in the file to be sure that the answers submitted by the client are true and correct to the best of his knowledge.

4) When they have been prepared in final form, either have the client come in and sign the final draft and verification form; or else mail a copy of the final typed version with a verification form to the client for review and signature.

5) Finally, file the original with the court, with a copy to the opposing side, and retain a copy for your files.

C) *Plaintiff Procedure*—Request for Admissions:

1) In developing your Request for Admissions, determine what it is your attorney wants admitted or accomplished by this discovery vehicle, then review the Complaint, Answer to Complaint, and Answers to Interrogatories (if applicable).

2) *Defendant:* If you are the recipient of Requests for Admissions, you should be guided by your attorney in preparing the answers.

3) Once the answers have been prepared and approved by your attorney, obtain the client's signature in the same way as for the answers to interrogatories set forth above.

D) *Depositions:*

1) From the answers to the interrogatories and/or Request for Admissions, your attorney will have determined if he wants to depose a witness or a party to the action; or if there is a need for production and copying or inspection of documents. To this end, you should do one of the following: you can set a deposition by way of oral argument; you can set a deposition by stipulation; or you can set a deposition on notice.

*Note*: Non-party depositions must be subpoenaed first. This procedure may vary from state to state, so please check your local code section for the typical procedure in your state.

Finally, consider two other major vehicles of discovery— PRODUCTION OF DOCUMENTS AND OBJECTS AND PHYSICAL AND MENTAL EXAMINATION OF LITIGANT (usually the plaintiff.)

## A. PRODUCTION OF DOCUMENTS—
## NOTICE AND MOTION

If discovery is to be used at all and your attorney is to be successful in the trial of an action, you must be aware of the existence of any pertinent documentation relevant to the subject matter of the lawsuit. Your attorney must have physical custody of copies of any and all documents.

## How Do You Obtain These Documents?

These documents would have been discovered via the use of the interrogatory or deposition discovery vehicles. If so discovered, you can move for their production, copying and inspection through the use of a Notice to Produce compelling a party to produce relevant documents for inspection; or, force a party-litigant or non-party to permit inspection of tangible evidence such as machinery, real property, etc.; or by using a Notice of Deposition requesting a party-litigant to produce certain documents at the deposition; or, through use of a Subpoena Duces Tecum re Deposition requiring a witness to bring such documents to his deposition.

## Step-by-Step Tactical Procedures

The following step-by-step procedures should be checked with your local court rules before you proceed.

1. Cause the subpoena duces tecum and affidavit to be served on the witness within a reasonable time before his appearance, this reasonable time being governed by local custom and practice;

2. Cause the subpoena duces tecum and affidavit to be filed with the court within the time prescribed by local court rules prior to the date of the scheduled appearance by the witness;

3. *A proven measure:* Though not mandatory, serve a copy of the affidavit and the subpoena duces tecum on any and all parties to the litigation.

The notice and motion should specify what documents are required for production and inspection (and for copying) and should specify the time and place at which the same are to be accomplished. This notice and motion should be accompanied by a supporting declaration which spells out, with specificity and clarity, good cause supporting the discovery requested, together with a memorandum of points and authorities in support thereof.

## The VIP Pleading

The key to a successful motion for production of documents is the declaration in support of a subpoena duces tecum. This affidavit or declaration should be as complete as possible and include the following:

1. The specific items requested in detail to make it necessary for the custodian of records to identify and obtain the documents you need or want;

2. A description of each document and why the same is material to your case and how production is relevant and necessary;

3. Facts supporting why the discovery should be permitted and,

4. It must state that the documents requested are under the exclusive control and possession of the person being deposed.

## B. PHYSICAL AND MENTAL EXAMINATION— NOTICE AND MOTION

This notice and motion is primarily used in personal injury, medical malpractice and Workmen's Compensation litigation, as it is in these types of lawsuits primarily that the mental and physical condition of a litigant have become an issue. As a legal assistant you should, therefore, be acquainted with an expert in the medical field pertinent to the injury to be used prior to, and at the time of, trial.

### Step-by-Step Procedure for Filing Motion

This physical and/or mental examination can be obtained by making a motion, on notice as prescribed by law, to be served on all parties. It should be accompanied by a declaration stating the reason for the request (the showing of good cause) and a memorandum of points and authorities in support thereof.

The physician performing the examination is required to submit a detailed, narrative report which, in a Workmen's Compensation case, is to be served on all parties; and in a personal injury or medical malpractice case, mailed, upon request, to the party examined. To this end, the party being examined should submit any previous medical reports and X-rays for the use and benefit of said physician. This is the role of a legal assistant.

*Note*: Even if the physician files a report, you can still take his deposition. As a general rule, the purpose of this type of motion for a physical or mental examination, is to secure a copy of a doctor's findings and conclusions after examination; or where the defendant has determined that the injuries complained of or sustained by plaintiff are not as severe as indicated.

As a plaintiff-legal assistant you should be aware that your client must comply with any request for a physical or mental examination. Having made his mental or physical condition an issue (or issues) in the lawsuit, he has waived whatever privilege existed pertinent thereto.

In developing your interrogatories, consider the following form as well as the topics to be covered in questioning the defendant, as set forth on the first form of interrogatories for wrongful death.

If you are the recipient of interrogatories from a defendant, then consider the following sample objections to those interrogatories. These objections, of course, should be discussed with your attorney before you attempt to utilize them.

The above comments are pertinent to the following form entitled Request for Admissions; and as indicated in the discussion heretofore set forth, this form and its contents should be thoroughly discussed with your attorney prior to their utilization by you.


INTERROGATORIES PROPOUNDED BY DEFENDANT
(WRONGFUL DEATH)

Attorney for Defendant.

) NO. _____
)
) INTERROGATORIES
)
) PROPOUNDED BY DEFENDANT
)
) (Wrongful Death)
_____.)


Defendant, pursuant to Sections _____ and _____, Code of Civil Procedure,* requests that the following interrogatories be answered under oath, separately and fully, within 20 days by _____.

Deborah E. Larbalestrier

_____
Attorney for Defendant.

---

*Your applicable Code Sections.

*Scope:* It is intended by these interrogatories to elicit information not only within your own personal knowledge but obtainable by you, including information in possession of your attorney, investigators, insurance carriers and their representatives. Whenever the term "accident" is used, it refers to the accident or incident which is the subject matter of your lawsuit.

If you cannot answer the following interrogatories in full, after exercising due diligence-to secure the information to do so, so state, and answer the remainder, stating whatever information or knowledge you have concerning the unanswered portions.

A. FUNERAL AND BURIAL EXPENSES ....
B. ILLNESSES, INJURIES AND USE OF TOBACCO, LIQUOR AND DRUGS BEFORE THE ACCIDENT SUED UPON....
C. EMPLOYMENT OF DECEDENT, PAST AND AT THE TIME OF DEATH....
D. INJURIES AND MEDICAL EXPENSES OF DECEDENT AT OR NEAR THE TIME OF DEATH....
E. DAMAGES CLAIMED BY SURVIVOR, INCLUDING ANTICIPATED FUTURE BENEFITS FROM THE DECEDENT AND SERVICES TO SURVIVORS....
F. COSTS OF SUPPORT REGARDING THE DECEDENT, THE DECEDENT'S NET WORTH AND LIFE EXPECTANCY OF THE DECEDENT....
G. INSURANCE....

## TWELVE SAMPLE OBJECTIONS
## TO INTERROGATORIES

1. RELEVANCE (Basic)

   *Objection:* The question is not calculated to lead to the discovery of information relevant to the subject matter of this action.

2. RELEVANCE (Broad & Remote)

   *Objection:* The question is overly broad and remote and as such is not calculated to lead to the discovery of information which is relevant to the subject matter of this action.

3. RELEVANCE (Indefinite Time)

   *Objection:* The question is remote and indefinite as to time and consequently is not calculated to lead to the discovery of information which is relevant to the subject matter of this action.

4. OPPRESSION (Indefinite Time)

   *Objection:* To answer this question would result in annoyance, embarrassment, or oppression to plaintiff in that the question is overly broad, indefinite as to time and without reasonable limitation in its scope.

5. WORK
PRODUCT
(I.D. of Ex-
pert Witness)

*Objection:* Attorney's work product privilege.
Plaintiff has not yet decided on which, if any, expert
witnesses may be called at trial. Any experts utilized
by plaintiff to date are for purposes of consultation
and case preparation.

6. OPPRESSION
(Legal)
Analysis)

*Objection:* Oppressive, harassing and burdensome;
the information sought requests plaintiff's counsel
to provide legal analysis and review for defendant
when the laws, ordinances, safety orders, etc., are
equally available to the parties.

7. OPPRESSIVE
(Boilerplate)

*Objection:* The question is boilerplate in form,
requiring reference back to the preceding questions
or introductions, thus making the questions oppressive, burdensome, ambiguous and unintelligible.

8. OPPRESSIVE
(Ambigous-
Speculation)

*Objection:* The question is oppressive and burdensome
because it is vague, ambiguous, and unintelligible so
as to make a response impossible without speculation
as to the meaning of the question.

9. OPPRESSIVE
(Equally
available
info.)

*Objection:* The question calls for information which
is not in plaintiff's possession, and which is available to all parties equally, and is therefore oppressive and burdensome.

10. ASKED &
ANSWERED

*Objection:* Asked and answered in prior interrogatories;
to wit:

11. ATTY-CLIENT
PRIVILEGE
(General)

*Objection:* Attorney-client privilege protects disclosure of the information sought.

12. WORK
PRODUCT
(Trial
Witnesses)

*Objection:* The question seeks disclosure of trial
witnesses (other than experts) and is therefore
violative of the attorney work product privilege.

REQUEST FOR ADMISSIONS (UNDER RULE 36)

Attorney Information

Court Information

| | | |
|---|---|---|
| Plaintiff, ) | Case No. _____ _____ | |
| ) | | |
| vs. ) | **REQUESTS FOR ADMISSIONS** | |
| ) | (Under Rule 36) | |
| ) | | |
| Defendant. ) | | |
| _____ ) | | |

Plaintiff requests that defendant within _____ days after service of this request, make the following admissions for the purpose of this action only, and subject to all pertinent objections as to admissibility which may be interjected at the trial.

1. That each of the following documents, exhibited with this request, are genuine (here, indented, you should list all the documents and describe them with clarity).

2. That each of the following statements is true (here should be listed the following statements you want admitted and they should be stated in such a way that you can get a clear yes or no answer).

DATED: _____

_____
Attorney

Following are examples of the various ways in which you can digest a deposition; however, even these formats should be governed by the policy and desires of your attorney.

Note that the first one is a narrative summary of a deposition, noting in parens at the end of each paragraph the page and line.

The second form of a deposition digest is equally a narrative deposition, but set up in a different format in that the page numbers are placed in the margin with cross-references incorporated within each as to another defendant witness.

## DEPOSITION SUMMARY OF MARGARET HEIDT TAKEN ON
## OCTOBER 16, 19___

She has resided in _____, _____, for 14 years. She lives with her husband and has three children. None of the children live with her. She is 48 years old on the date of deposition. (70: 2-15).

In the accident she broke her left hip. She broke her leg between the knee and the foot. She broke three lower vertebrae in her back. She has numerous broken ribs on both sides of her body. She had some trouble with her bladder, in that she had a bleeding which lasted for about three months. She fractured her pelvis. It was broken in four or five places. She had lacerations on her forehead in the upper left portion. Stitches were taken, approximately 3 or 4. She knocked a tooth loose in the accident, and she had problems with her neck. (70: 25-72:15).

The problems in the neck caused Mrs. Heidt to black out if she turned her head in a certain position, even when she was lying down. It started in the hospital in _____. The doctor did not tell Mrs. Heidt she had a neck injury, but they x-rayed the neck to find out if there was something wrong which casued the blacking out. They couldn't determine whether or not there was. When she turned her head to the right and back she would black out completely. She doesn't know how long she stayed out, probably for minutes. Her blood pressure would drop. She had the problem until June of 1969. From that time until the time of deposition she had no recurrence of that. (72: 17-73: 22). She also had problems with her eyes; if she was seeing something white, there would be a black speck in front of it. (73: 25-74:1).

She was rendered unconscious in the accident. The last thing she remembers before being rendered unconscious was a red light and then a green light. They seemed to be directly in front of her or to the left. (74: 10-16).

She remembers being at the Golden Cock Restaurant. She remembers coming out of the restaurant to the parking lot and the car. She was seated in the car on the right side in the front. The vehicle was equipped with seat belts. She was not wearing one. They turned to the left when the car came out of the parking lot. She did not remember crossing a highway to get to the left. (74: 10-75:5). She does not know how far they traveled from the parking lot driveway until the accident. She would estimate half a block. She states she was not tired before the accident, but emotionally upset. She was not sleepy. (75: 9-15).

## NARRATIVE DEPOSITION WITH CROSS REFERENCE
### DEPOSITION OF ***********

Page

7    On October 8, 197_ in the evening, he had about
     three bourbon and soda drinks. He paid for those
     dirnks in cash. (Cross reference to deposition in
     _____ case: At page 20, he appears to have paid
     for drinks on credit. Also, in daily summary sheets
     of the bar, he had tab of three drinks.)

13   He stopped for a red traffic light at Parthenia and
     Reseda Boulevard when he was going northbound on
     Reseda Boulevard. (Cross-reference: Page 26 of
     his deposition in _____ case states that he does
     not remember if he stopped at any lights from the
     intersection of Roscoe and Reseda to the place of
     the accident).

15   He does not know whether or not the vehicle his
     truck hit was moving or stopped at the time of the
     impact.

16   He changed to the Number 1 lane from the Number 2 lane
     of Reseda Boulevard somewhere in the neighborhood of
     approximately half a block before the intersection
     of Prairie and Reseda. When he changed from the
     Number 2 lane to the Number 1 lane, he was going
     about 35 miles per hour.

17   (Contradicts statement on page 16) He was travel-
     ing very slowly, say 15 to 20, when he changed lanes.
     He clarified by stating that when he did get into
     the Number 1 lane he traveled at about 35 miles
     per hour. He changed from the Number 2 lane into
     the Number 1 lane to get around the slow vehicle
     in front of him in the Number 2 lane.

18   Once he got into the Number 1 lane, he accelerated
     to approximately 35 miles per hour.
     He does not know whether or not the vehicle he hit
     was in the intersection or south of the intersec-
     tion, or whether it was moving or stopped.

### DEPOSITION OF *******

No information in her deposition was of any significance to our case.
Her statements relalated mostly to her personal injuries as a result of the
accident.

# Working with a Probate File

# CHAPTER 6

*This chapter gives you the tools to perform preventive law in estate planning; as well as probating the estate of your client, be it the Last Will and Testament or a guardianship or conservatorship proceeding.*

## INTRODUCTION

Estate planning deals primarily with rights and duties; human needs and emotions; love and hate; fairness and equity; and the professional lawyer is the mediator. It is his job to help the client plan for the distribution of his property either during his lifetime or after his death—the giving away of the property he has worked all his life to obtain.

Hence, estate planning also entails anxiety, involvement and the need to do the right things for heirs and descendants. The job of a legal assistant, therefore, is to make this procedure more competent, and to make the procedure more competent is to know what facts should be gathered, how they should be gathered and what documents need to be prepared in order to expedite this emotional time for the client.

To an attorney with a heavy estate planning and probate practice, you, as a legal assistant specially trained in the procedure for estate planning, probate and estate administration, are an invaluable asset, since much of the attorney's valuable time normally spent dealing with a client in a probate matter can be delegated to you.

Generally, your duties would be as follows:

1. Interviewing clients, gathering facts and assembling assets to prepare a will or for the probate of the will;
2. Drafting the inventory and appraisement documents;
3. Researching the tax laws applicable;

4. Developing financial data for filing the appropriate state and federal tax forms;

5. Preparing memoranda for estate planning and administration;

6. Drafting trust agreements; and

7. Auditing and up-dating wills to keep the attorney and client abreast of changes.

## WILLS

### Introduction

The underlying purpose in having a will prepared is to prevent the State from imposing its will upon the estate of a testator. If a deceased person had not prepared a will, the State in which he resided at the time of his death would have one prepared for him. This is the law of Intestate Succession. In this estate, however, the disposition of a property is not what the testator or his heirs may have wanted or desired. A will is designed to express the desire and intent of a testator for the disposition of his real and personal property.

Because of a change in the laws and applicable taxes affecting gifts and trusts relating to the disposition of a testator's property, one of the duties of a legal assistant would be that of urging a client to come in every so often for a ''legal checkup'' in this area. This is commonly called ''preventive law.''

### Developing Wills

In estate planning, probate and estate administration, you will basically be dealing with wills, codicils, trust agreements, and the probate procedures after the death of a testator(trix). In connection therewith, recall the following:

1) There is the formal, witness will;

2) The holographic will[1], which must be totally in the handwriting of the testator to be valid, including signature and date on which it was written and signed; and

---

[1]Note that this form of Will is only valid as to personal property, and in some jurisdictions it is not recognized at all. You should consult your local state statutes for clarification as to the use and validity of a holographic will and the procedure for probating the same.

3) The nuncupative which is an oral statement reduced to writing (within the prescribed statutory time limit) by the person who heard the testator make the statement.[2]

*Remember:* All of the foregoing wills can be broken down into mutual and joint wills, if applicable and valid in your state.

## Key Elements of a Will

1) Introduction which incorporates the identity of ......

    (a) testator and the document;

    (b) testator's family and definitions, if any;

    (c) instructions as to the payment of his last debts.

2) Legacies which incorporate:

    (a) property not accounted for or given away;

    (b) special gifts to identified individuals, (such as "my 1979 car to Mary Smith''); and

    (c) gifts to charity.

3) Simplicity of draftmanship in:

    (a) appointment of executor and alternate;

    (b) spelling out of the power of executor and/or trustee;

    (c) closing out the will, including statement and signature of testator and witnesses, at least 2 (or more if required in your state).

## Checklist for Determining a Valid Will

1. The will must have been executed with testamentary intent.
2. The testator must have had testamentary capacity. That is, he must have had the ability at the time the will was drawn and executed to do that which he intended.
3. The execution, assuming capacity, must be done or had without fraud, undue influence, duress and the like.
4. The will must have been duly executed and be in compliance with statutory requirements.

---

[2]This Will could be a deathbed statement of intent or a battlefield expression and the like, and it is only applicable to nominal or minimal assets of personal property. Here again, you should consult your state statutes, since the treatment of nuncupative wills varies from state to state. For example, in Alabama the holographic will is not even recognized.

## The Codicil

As you know, a codicil is a subsequently drawn document which can be a part of the original will, or a separate document in place of the original will; and the same may revoke a portion of or amend a previously drawn will; or it may just name an executor.

*Remember:* A codicil can publish a will; it can and may invalidate a prior will, or make valid that which has become a "revoked prior will."

## Vital Legal Checkups

In drafting wills and codiciles, be careful about the date of the codicil:

### FOR EXAMPLE:

If a testator makes a will *before marriage* as to his real and personal property, and does not make a codicil *after he is married,* the wife is entitled to one-half of the property.[3]

It is therefore to the advantage of the testator to make a will, either confirming his marriage and his wife's entitlement to half of his real and personal property, or disinheriting her as to his separate property owned before his marriage.

Further, watch out for ambiguities in your codicils. Patent ambiguities appear obvious on the face of the document, but the latent ambiguities do not.

### FOR EXAMPLE:

In changing the house devise to be, when the testator has in fact sold the house referred to in his will, and has since purchased another house, you should spell out the house with specificity, giving the legal description and the common street address.

## Revoking a Will or Codicil

The time may arise when your client may want to revoke his codicil or his will—in any of the following ways:

1) By the execution of a new formal will;
2) By drawing a codicil which is inconsistent with the original will;

---

[3]Check local code to determine the applicability of this procedure in your state.

3) By burning or physically destroying the will or codicil;

4) By a change in the circumstances of the testator, such as marriage.

## Affect of Change in Marital Status—Before and After

EXAMPLE

Alice and Boyd marry and make wills, leaving property to each other. At the time of the dissolution of the marriage, generally speaking, if the dissolution is the result of a legal proceeding, gifts from one spouse to another as contained in a will, will be invalidated unless there is some language in the will making it clear that the testator intends to give the gift regardless of whether or not he is divorced.

*Note:* In many states the entire will is not revoked by divorce.
It is therefore best to urge clients who have filed divorce proceedings to rewrite their wills, or at least codicils to their wills, changing their beneficiary and leaving only the spousal rights required under the laws of intestate succession and such other rights as provided by law. IT SAVES A LOT OF HEADACHES LATER ON.

However, this change or possibility is sometimes covered in a property settlement agreement, wherein you have stated that each spouse, among other things, shall have no interest in the other's estate, or take any inheritance. This document will normally evolve itself into having this type of effect. It repudiates and/or surrenders any right of a gift in the testator's will. In California, however, it is not a valid instrument as to the will.

It is a contrasting aspect of the property settlement agreement which revokes the will, not the divorce per se. It is not, however, applicable to the children of the parties unless the testator specifically writes them out of his will. As a legal assistant, you should be aware of the client's change in status or circumstances and up-date his will accordingly.

## WORKING WITH A PROBATE FILE
## I. INITIAL STEPS YOU SHOULD TAKE
## AS TO ALL PROBATE ADMINISTRATION

As to both intestate and testate proceedings, remember to do the following:

a) Search for burial instructions and/or Will to dispose of a body;

b) If applicable, open safe deposit box for burial instructions and/or Will;

c) Determine if a special administrator is needed;

d) Have copies made of Will for later use in the administration procedure;

e) Locate witnesses to Will; or, if it is a holographic Will, someone who can prove the handwriting of the decedent;

f) Prepare documentation for initiating the estate, including Petition for Probate of Will and Letters Testamentary, Petition for Probate of Will, and for Letters of Administration with Will Annexed, Petition for Probate of Lost or Destroyed Will, Petition for Letters of Administration in an Intestate Estate, Petition for Special Letters of Administration, and the like, whichever is applicable.

g) Determine who is to be the petitioner; and,

h) Ascertain names, addresses, agent of heirs-at-law, and/or beneficiaries.

## Introduction of Definitions

The following definitions are set forth herein below to aid you in utilizing the information in the Sections that follow:

1. Intestate refers to an individual who has died without making a will; or without leaving anything to testify what his wishes were with respect to the dispostion of his property after death.

2. Testate refers to one who has made a will; one who has died leaving a will which sets forth his desires as to the disposition of his property after his death.

# II. PROBATING THE ESTATE

## A. Intestate—Step-by-Step Procedures

1) File Petition for Letters of Administration;

2) Prepare and file Notice of Hearing.

*Helpful Hint:* Be sure any and all heirs, or suspected heirs, are notified of the hearing date by registered mail with return receipt requested, at least two (2) days (or whatever statutory period of time is required by your local state rules) prior to the date of the hearing in order to forestall any litigated contest of the Will.

3) File any contest to petitioner, petitioning for Letters of Administration.

*Proven Tactical Measures:* In preparing your boss for the hearing, remember to authenticate testimony to establish death of the decedent (by a death certificate, and such). Further, be sure to document residency requirements as per your local state codes. And finally, have gathered together all documentation relative to known and unknown heirs.

4) Prepare an Order Appointing the Administrator (an original and three (3) copies) to be placed in your attorney's file so he will have them with him on the date of the hearing in court;

5) Prepare Letters of Administration. These, too, should be prepared before the hearing and placed in your attorney's file. You should make an original and three (3) copies initially, with additional copies to be secured when and as needed.

## B. Administering the Estate: (Intestate)

In administering the estate you should be aware of and complete the following tasks:

a) Publicize a Notice to Creditors. Calendar the date they were mailed, since all claims should be filed within four (4) months from the date of publication. (This statutory limitation may be different in your state. You are therefore cautioned to check your local court rules as to this time period);

b) If applicable in your state, request of the court an appointment of an appraiser, otherwise, in some jurisdictions it is done automatically by the court;

c) Important! Prepare an original and three (3) copies of an Inventory and Appraisement. Be sure that you have kept a fully executed copy of this document in your file.

*Note*: As to each of the above-referred to documents, be sure that the petitioner has signed in all the spaces provided for his or her signature.

d) Duties and powers of an administrator are peculiar to each estate and in line with your local court rules and state policies, hence, the following is submitted as a reminder and as an overview of what these powers and duties should be:

1) Liquidate assets;

2) Raise funds by selling property and/or collecting outstanding debts due to the estate;

3) Pay all outstanding debts as soon as possible, which should include state and federal taxes as well as any inheritance taxes, and

4) Pay all affixed administration and attorney's fee, if applicable.

## C. Distribution and Settlement of Estate: (Intestate)

Often, it is required that some sort of preliminary distribution is mandatory or necessary. If so, then be governed by the rules and regulations of the court rules in the area, as well as by state policy. As a general proposition, however, final distribution procedures are as follows:

1) After the statutory limitation period has expired from date of first publication of Notice to Creditors you can begin to distribute to the heirs and legatees that which is allotted to them under the Will;

2) There should be prepared a Current and Final Accounting prior to the final distribution to the heirs;

3) If the First and Final Accounting is approved by the court, then your attorney can distribute the funds in the estate as set forth under the Will or trust agreement;

4) Thereafter, file application to the court for final discharge of the petitioner, the executor, and your attorney; and

5) File Application for Termination of Proceeding when the estate is exhausted. It should be noted that this document should be signed by both the executor and the attorney.

## D. Testate—Step-by-Step Procedures

1) File the Petition to Probate Will and for Letters Testamentary (or for Letters of Administration Annexed, if appropriate).

*Note*: In your state you may have a similar or like document under a different title or heading. You are therefore cautioned to check your local probate court rules to determine which form is applicable.

2) Send out Notice of Hearing to all named heirs, beneficiaries, etc., as well as those unknown;

3) Prepare documentation for issuance of your Letters before the hearing date so that the attorney may have the same in his files.

> a) Prepare your Order for Letters Testamentary;
>
> b) Have documented Subscribing Witness Affidavits and Proof of Will.

*Caution:* In some states this procedure has been changed, and a printed document is now used; further, in some states a certified copy of the original Will must be submitted to the witness for verification as to the signature. Please check your local rules in this regard.

> c) Prepare Order Admitting Will to Probate;
>
> d) Secure a bond, if required or applicable.

## E. Administration of the Testate Estate

a) Use the same procedures as set forth under General Outline for Probating an Estate where there is no Will;

b) Paragraphs (1) through (5) of paragraph C regarding distribution and settlement of an intestate estate can be utilized here. However, please check your local rules to be sure that this is true in your state.

## F. Chronological Step-by-Step Procedure in Handling a Conservatorship: Definition

A *conservator:* is a person appointed to take care of a person and property, or person or property of a conservatee.

1. Collect and organize data needed to set up a conservatorship.
2. Compile Petition for appointment of conservator.
3. Prepare Order for citation.
4. Prepare citation.
5. Prepare acceptance of service of citation and waiver.
6. Write document needed to place under conservator.
7. Write court order appointing conservator.
8. Document inventory of assets under conservatorship.
9. Administer conservator checking account.
10. Provide annual accounting for conservatorship.
11. Compile tax returns affected by conservatorship.
12. Write court order approving annual accounting.
13. Compile conservatorship final accounting.

14. Write court order approving conservatorship final accounting and direct distribution.
15. Fill out conservatorship direct distribution sheet.
16. Write court order closing conservatorship.
17. Prepare a conservator's petition for sale of real property.
18. Prepare and serve citation for sale.
19. Write court order to sell real property under conservatorship.
20. Write conservator's petition for sale of personal property.
21. Write court order to sell personal property under conservatorship.

## G. Suggested Step-by-Step Procedures in Handling the Following

MINORS

*Definition:* Guardian: is the person appointed to take care of a person or property of another, who is called the ward of the guardian. Note that Letters of Guardianship may also be applied for as they relate to minors and/or incompetents.

1. File petition for Letters of Guardianship.
2. Send out notices of hearing to interested parties.
3. Prepare for hearing:
   (a) Order appointing guardian;
   (b) Letters of guardianship;
   (c) Secure bond, if required.

INCOMPETENTS

1. File petition for Letters of Guardianship.
2. Send out notice of hearing to all interested parties, including relatives, creditors, etc.;
3. Prepare for hearing:
   (a) Order appointing guardian;
   (b) Letters of guardianship;
   (c) Bond, if required.

## H. Recapitulation of the General Functional Duties in Working with a Probate File

1) Interview and gather information on finances;
2) Redeem or re-issue savings bonds and arrange for collection of insurance proceeds;

3) Assist in collection of death benefits from Social Security and annuities;

4) Prepare documentation for compliance with summary administration procedures;

5) Prepare documentation for transfer of joint tenancy personal property and termination of joint tenancy real property;

6) Assist in marshalling, transferring and distribution of estate assets;

7) Prepare documentation for appointment of inheritance tax referee, personal representative to appraise assets and prepare inventory and appraisement;

8) Handle presentation, filing, compromise and payment of creditors' claims, including notices and publications;

9) Prepare miscellaneous documentation, such as for sales of estate property, including real property, personal property, perishable or depreciating property securities;

10) Prepare documentation for continuance of business, lease of real property, conveyance of real property, transfer of personal property;

11) Prepare documentation for ancillary administration, for probating foreign will, and distributing assets to domiciliary representative;

12) Prepare documentation for closing estate, including determining interests in estate distribution, partitioning before distribution, preliminary (partial or interim) distribution, accountings, final account, distribution and discharge, and fees and commissions;

13) Close files and reopen estates after distribution;

14) Draft forms for State Inheritance Tax, Federal Estate Tax, State and Federal Income Tax and Fiduciary Income Tax.

FORM

WILL (WRITTEN/TYPED)

I, a resident of the City of _____, County of _____, State of _____, and residing at _____ Street, being of the age of majority; of sound and disposing mind and memory, and not acting under duress, menace, fraud or undue influence, do make, publish and declare this to be my Last Will and Testament.

FIRST: I direct all my debts, including my funeral expenses and the expense of my last illness together with expenses of the administration of my estate be paid by my executor to be named hereafter out of the first monies coming to his or her hands and available therefor.

SECOND: I hereby declare that I am married; my wife's (husband's) name is _____, that I have ____ children, (then set forth the names of each child, together with their birthdate).

THIRD: I give, devise and bequeath all of the rest and residue of my property, after the payment of the debts and expenses hereinabove provided for, be it real, personal or mixed, of whatever kind of character, and wheresoever situated to my _____.

FOURTH: I hereby nominate and appoint _____ the executor of this, my Last Will and Testament.

FIFTH: I hereby revoke all former Wills and Codicils to Wills heretofore by me made.

IN WITNESS WHEREOF, I have hereunto set my hand and seal this _____ day of _____, 19__.

_____
Testator (trix)

(*Note:* In some states, it is required that a seal be attached following the name of testator or testatrix).

The foregoing instrument, consisting of ____ pages beside this, was at the date hereof, by _____, signed, sealed and published as, and declared to be his (or her) Last Will and Testament in the presence of us, who at his (or her) request and in his (her) presence and in the presence of each other, have signed our names as witnesses hereto.

_____

_____

FORM

FORM OF ADMINISTRATION (ANCILLARY)

KNOW ALL MEN BY THESE PRESENTS, that _____ of the County and State of _____, died on the _____ day of _____, 19__, at _____, in the City and State of _____, leaving a Will which has been duly proved and probated in the County of _____, State of _____, and I, _____, of the City and State of _____, have been duly appointed as executor (trix) of that Will.

And whereas the testator left goods and estate to be administered in the State of _____, all of which he devised and bequeathed to his executor (trix) in trust.

BY THESE PRESENTS:

I appoint _____ of the City and State of _____, as my attorney, to apply for and obtain in his own name from the proper court in the County and State of _____, Letters of Administration with Will Annexed, limited to the property of the testator wherever situated in the City, County and State of _____, and for this purpose to execute and deliver such bond or other obligation as may be required upon the grant of such Letters of Administration.

And further, as administrator of the property (here the legal assistant should set forth all the rights of this appointed administrator in administrating this estate which could be some of the following: The right to sue and/or enforce payment of debts; to discharge all monies and goods which belong to the deceased or may hereinafter belong to the deceased; which may be due and owing to the estate from any person or entity; and this administrator may have the right or be given the right to take and retain property, receive rents and/or profits from property in the City and State so designated.)

(The last paragraph should be ''In Witness, etc.'' type of closing.)

---

## Acknowledgment

The legal assistant should check with her attorney to see if there are any other general clauses that the attorney might wish to include.

# Working with Corporate Matters

*In order to set up a business entity, you need to know all the underlying factors that go into establishing a successful business. This chapter is designed to give you that edge.*

# CHAPTER 7

## INTRODUCTION

Remember that the business entity is a legal entity which has been granted the right to do business in a particular state or country—and this right is evidenced by the filing with the appropriate authorities of a corporate charter or articles of incorporation. You will recall that in some states, this document is called a Certificate of Incorporation. This Certificate of Incorporation may be amended by the filing of a Certificate of Amendment, or Articles of Amendment.

Just in case you are asked to do the initial interviewing of a client wishing to set up a business entity, recall the following factors which set forth the advantages of such a legal entity:

1. Limited liability of shareholders.
2. Lower tax rate on profits.
3. The perpetual existence of a legal entity.
4. The transferability of the shares of stock.
5. The ease in raising capital, and so forth.

*Note*: This may sound like legal advice, but it is not. It is legal information which you have derived from either working on other cases or listening to your boss talk to other clients. It is considered general information.

## ORGANIZING THE BUSINESS ENTITY

### Tactical Steps:—Key Factors You Should Determine Prior to Setting Up a Business Entity.

1) How much money will you need?
2) What is the liability of a sole proprietor or general partnership involved?
3) Is there a transferability of interest?
4) Legal status:
   a) Can the proposed entity hold property?
   b) Can the proposed entity transfer ownership?
   c) Can the proposed entity sue or be sued?
5) Longevity. Will the debts of/or withdrawal by a partner terminate the business?
6) Abilities of the promoters. Are they professional?
7) Can they provide capital?
8) Are they experienced in business management?
9) What are the tax ramifications of the business entity?

### HYPOTHETICAL FACTS

Bill Jones comes to your office seeking advice and recommendation from your attorney relative to the organization of a business entity. He is the current sole proprietor of a bookstore and desires to expand his business to include partners or perhaps set up a corporation. He wants your office to advise him as to the needs of such a venture in the area of capitalization, how to go about obtaining the required financing, such as stock issuance, and so forth. Simply put, he wants to know whether or not he should change from being a sole proprietor to becoming a "corporate officer."

### Practical Checklists for Collecting the Information

1) Secure or obtain from client proposed name and location of his business;
2) The purpose of the business;
3) The track record for his current business;
4) Obtain a brief profile of the client and other proposed incorporators;

5) How much capitalization he feels he needs with a projection; and

6) Determine from the client (and check yourself with the local courts) as to whether or not there is any pending litigation involving the client, his business or the proposed partners or incorporators.

## Tried and Proven Hint

The memorandum to your attorney should include the following:

1) A recapitulation of the facts;

2) All of the information collected from the above-described checklist;

3) An outline of the results of your research relating to alternative methods for financing, such as selling stock, exchanging stock for services, loans via small investment firms, large public underwriting companies, banking institutions or private financing;

4) A breakdown of the tax ramifications applicable;

5) A summarization of the above, together with your recommendation; and

6) Any and all exhibits you feel would be appropriate.

## ARTICLES OF INCORPORATION

The Articles of Incorporation, as you know, is a boilerplate document in most states. Please be aware that in some states they have been reduced to include just the following:

A. All you require is the name of the corporation;

B. State a succinct purpose, and/or business of the intended corporation;

C. Name with specificity the agent qualified to receive service of process; and finally,

D. The nature of the stock to be issued on behalf of the corporation.

## MECHANICS' LIENS

### Introduction

A corporate office handles clients in the building or construction industry. In such a firm, you will be exposed to stop notices, notices of completion, mechanics' liens, etc. Therefore, you must know the elements of, and the procedures in, defending a complaint to foreclose a mechanic's lien; as well as the importance of the accuracy of statute of limitation dates in compliance with the laws governing mechanics' liens. You will be required to review the terms of the original contract, the timing, filing and recordation of the various notices and the service of these documents upon the parties involved in the transaction.

> *Caution:* Don't forget to check your local statutes and the rules and regulations of the office of the recorder so that you can comply with the time table therein set forth in filing these stop notices, completions, certifications and so forth, since they may vary from state to state.

### Systems Vary

The two prevailing systems applicable to mechanics' liens are as follows:

The *New York System* which states that the right to file a mechanic's lien is dependent upon the indebtedness of the owner of the property to the general contractor, after service of notice that labor, material and so forth have been furnished. This is commonly referred to as a derivative lien.

The *Pennsylvania System,* on the other hand, states that the laborer, subcontractor or other such individual has a direct lien which is not dependent on the indebtedness of the owner of the property to the general contractor.

It is suggested, therefore, that you check your local statute to determine which "system" governs your state.

> *Note*: In the above referenced material, mention should be made of a materialman's lien which refers to individuals who have furnished materials to be used in the construction or repair of buildings, structures, or vessels. Be aware that in most jurisdictions materialman's liens and the mechanic's liens are treated and processed similarly.

## SOME TIME RESTRICTIONS YOU SHOULD REMEMBER

### Notice of Completion (*)

Time within which to file a lien:

1) 60 days after completion of work by original contractor;

2) 30 days after completion of work by any claimant after he has ceased to perform labor or furnish materials. The filing of a Notice of Completion starts the time running for filing of a Notice of Mechanic's Lien.

If Notice of Completion is not filed, then,

1) Within 90 days after completion of said work to all persons.

### Notice of Cessation

If Notice of Cessation of Labor is filed by owners—after cessation of labor for a continuous period of 30 days or more, then

1) 60 days after filing the Notice by original contractor;

2) 30 days after filing of Notice by every person other than the original contractor.

If Notice of Cessation of Labor is not filed, then

1) Within 90 days from the expiration of cessation of labor, for a continuous period of 60 days.

* Check your local statutes as to this procedure to see if it is applicable in your state.

## STEP-BY-STEP PROCEDURE FOR ENFORCING A MECHANIC'S LIEN

1) Serve the Notice of Claim of Mechanic's Lien within the prescribed statutory time limitations on the construction lender; or

2) If applicable, on the reputed construction lender after the labor or services, or equipment and materials have been furnished.

This Notice should contain a general description of the work to be performed, and equipment and materials to be furnished; an estimate of the total price and a detailed description of the job site, etc.

*(Note:* This Notice should be sent by registered mail, return receipt requested.)

*Practical Hint:* If there is no construction lender as of the time of the contract date, then the Notice of Claim must be given within the prescribed statutory period to the owner of the property after the work of improvement has been commenced. You should check your local code as to the time restriction.

3) Record the lien with County Recorder within the required statutory period.

4) If settlement is reached, without a lawsuit being filed, record the release of the mechanic's lien; if not,

5) File a verified Complaint within 90 days (or other statutory limitation period) after recording the Notice of Claim of Mechanic's Lien;

6) Then record a Notice of Lis Pendens;

7) The balance of this procedure is the same as in any other civil action.

## In a Nutshell:

The basis for filing a Complaint to foreclose on a mechanic's lien may be as follows:

a) Breach of contract;

b) Breach of the terms of said contract which set forth the work to be performed;

c) Dispute as to what was intended to be performed and by whom;

d) The costs involved. (This cost could include "extra work."

## Tips

In defending a Complaint for foreclosure of a mechanic's lien:

1. Very carefully, scrutinize such things as the stop notices, notices of completion, the mechanic's lien itself, extra work orders, and so forth. This is to ensure the accuracy as to dates in compliance laws governing mechanics' liens, the term of the original contract and the timely filing and recordation of notices and services of said documents.

2. Always compare the incorporated and attached Notice of Claim and mechanic's lien with the one obtained by the title company, construction money lender, or Office of the County Recorder.

3. Pay particular attention to the date on which the same was filed and recorded, the description of the property being improved, the amount of money allegedly due and owing, and who signed it.

4. These points will aid you in filing the appropriate answer with affirmative defenses; or permit you to file a Demurrer to the Complaint; or Cross-complaint for damages.

## 21 FUNCTIONAL DUTIES OF A CORPORATE PARAPROFESSIONAL FORMING THE CORPORATION

### Basic Checklist

1) Check on availability of corporate name and reserve it;
2) Draft pre-incorporation subscriptions and consent forms for board of directors;
3) Draft and file Articles of Incorporation, Minutes of First Meeting of Board of Directors and corporate Bylaws;
4) Obtain minute book, seal and stock certificates;
5) Prepare documentation for opening corporate bank accounts;
6) Prepare and send notices of meetings and waivers;
7) Draft minutes of board of directors meetings and resolutions to be considered by board of directors, including those related to sales of stock, increase in capitalization, stock splits, stock options, pension plans, profit-sharing plans, election of officers, dividend distribution, spin-offs, liquidation and dissolution;
8) Maintain Articles and Bylaws by amendment and corporate minute book;
9) Draft agreements relating to employment, trade secrets, loans, notes, consulting, non-competition, stock restrictions, trusts and buy-sell;
10) Draft and maintain pension, profit-sharing and stock option plans;
11) Research statutory requirements for mergers and acquisitions, assist in gathering information and drafting of agreements for

merger and acquisition and in compliance with procedure of regulatory agencies;

12) Prepare documentation for dissolutions;

13) Prepare notices of annual and special shareholders meetings and assist in preparation of proxy materials, ballots and solicitations;

14) Prepare documentation for qualification to do business in a foreign jurisdiction;

15) Draft general and limited partnership agreements;

16) Draft and file statements and certificates of partnerships;

17) Prepare, file and have published fictitious business name statements;

18) Prepare minutes of partnership meetings;

19) Draft amendments to agreements, and agreements for dissolution;

20) Draft and file termination of fictitious business name;

21) Draft and file notice of termination of partnership.

## APPLICATION TO RESERVE CORPORATE NAME

_____
[Date]

To the Secretary of State
of the State of _____

    Pursuant to the provisions of Article 2:06 of the _____ Business Corporation Act, the undersigned hereby applies for reservation of the following corporate name for a period of one hundred twenty days:

    Dated: _____.

                       [_____]
                       BY _____


_____
[Date]

Charter Division
Office of Secretary of State
State of _____
_____, _____ 78711

    In Re: _____

Gentlemen:

    Please file the enclosed original and one copy of Application for Reservation of Corporate Name. We are enclosing our check in the amount of Ten Dollars ($10.00) to cover filing fees.

                       Very truly yours,

                       _____

Enclosures


## PLAN TO ISSUE SECTION 1244 STOCK*
### (IRC, Section 97,002)

    The following plan is based upon and made pursuant to the requirement of Section 1244 of the Internal Revenue Code and the regulations issued thereunder:

_____

*This 1244 Stock plan is no longer required under the law, and is submitted to help you in drafting whatever application is used in your office in applying for permission to issue stock.

1. The plan as herein set forth as adopted by the Board of Directors shall become effective upon the granting of a permit to issue securities by the _____ Corporations Commissioner (or the filing of a Section 25102 notice).

2. The Application for Permit to Issue Stock to be filed with the _____ Corporations Commissioner as set forth in the minutes of this corporation asks for authority to offer and issue _____ shares of common capital stock of $_____ par value and all such stock shall be issued in accordance with the terms of the Permit and in no event subsequent to 2 years following the granting of such Permit.

3. During the period set forth above in Paragraph 2, the Corporation shall offer and issue only such common capital stock and all such stock shall be issued pursuant to this plan.

4. Such common capital stock shall be issued only for *money* or *property other than stock and securities* and the maximum amount to be received by the Corporation in consideration of the stock to be issued pursuant to this plan shall be $_____.

5. Such other action shall be taken by the Corporation as shall qualify the stock offered and issued under this plan as ''Section 1244 stock'', as such term is defined in the Internal Revenue Code and the regulations issued thereunder.

Thereupon, upon motion duly made, seconded and unanimously carried, the following resolutions were passed:

RESOLVED, that the foregoing plan to issue Section 1244 stock be and the same is hereby adopted by the corporation, and it is

FURTHER RESOLVED, that the proper officers of this corporation be and are hereby authorized, empowered, and directed to do and perform any and all acts and deeds necessary to carry out such plan.


## STOCK STRUCTURE

The following stock structure is set up under the old 1244 Stock Plan and is submitted only to demonstrate how stock can be distributed and issued.

a.  Total number of shares of stock authorized:
    122,000
b.  Class of shares:  Two (2)
    Class A          Class B
c.  Number of shares authorized for each class and par value:
    Class A:      60,000 at $5 par
    Class B:      62,000 at $1 par
d.  Aggregate par value of all shares:
    $362,000
e.  Possible aggregate debt securities:
    $138,000

## CHECKLIST FOR THE
## CORPORATE PARAPROFESSIONAL

In setting up a corporation, be sure that you have determined the following:

1. Who will be the active directors in the corporation?

2. What major changes are expected in the future relative to active participation in the corporation?

3. Are the active parties expected to give loans in the future to the corporation; or will these funds be coming from outside sources as required?

4. Is the corporation to remain within and under the control of the initial promoters in the future?

5. Is each party willing to make full disclosure?

6. How do the parties plan to use the profits of the corporation—put it back into the corporation or take it out?

7. What is anticipated or planned for the profits or shares of a deceased or retiring partner?

8. Did you compute all fees necessary to incorporate?

9. Did you obtain the necessary licenses and permits, dba name statement, attorney's fees, record the certificate of limited partnership, qualifying fee, state recording and county clerk fees and purchase of notebook, seal and so forth?

10. Has an agent been appointed to accept service of process?

*Note*: Corporations can avoid direct service of process in California. However, there may be instances where it would be preferable to the corporation to designate such an agent. You should look to your local code for this or discuss this matter with your attorney.

11. Has the stock been issued and if so, have the shareholders been notified?

12. Determine that the minutes and bylaws have been prepared for signature by the appropriate parties.

13. Prepare adoption of a bylaws document showing if there were any restrictions and limitations on the adoption of the bylaws, if applicable.

14. Check to see that the adoption of the bylaws document has been executed.

15. Prepare permit to issue stock.

16. Issue the stock and be sure that the red ledger stock has been applied, if applicable.

17. Check to see if you have selected the date on which the corporation is to commence business or if it is an established business, when the income is to be shifted from the owners to the new corporation.

18. Check to determine if the date has been set for the new corporation to issue its shares of stock. (There is a question of legal liability involved in the issuance of stock, so be sure to check with your attorney as to the date on which these shares should be issued).

19. Check and determine if the date elected and desired for issuance of permit by your state commissioner of corporations is applicable.

20. Check to see if the date selected for filing the application to the commissioner of department of corporations for a permit to issue securities is applicable or required.

21. Check to see if you have set a firm date for the first meeting of the board of directors.

22. Determine if there is a definite date required for the filing of the articles of incorporation.

23. Determine if there is a definite date required for the reservation of the desired name for the new corporation. (There is a time limitation here so try to make your period for reserving a corporate name within the statutory limitation date, which in some states is 60 days, and file your request to coordinate with the selective date for filing the articles of incorporation).

24. Check and determine the date upon which your pre-incorporation subscription agreements should be executed. Be sure that this date falls within the statutory limitation, which is normally 90 days prior to the filing of the articles of incorporation. This statutory time limitation should be governed by the corporation rules and regulations of your state.

25. At the organizational meeting of the incorporating board of directors, be sure that dummy or straw directors file their resignations.

26. Check to be sure that you have filed a report with the secretary of state. This form is the one which should have been automatically mailed to you from the secretary of state when the articles of incorporation were filed. The name given to this document in California is entitled "Statement

by Domestic Corporation.'' You might look to your own local corporation rules and regulations to see if you have an applicable form document sent out by your local secretary of state.

The following forms are offered for illustrative purposes:

## STOP NOTICE TO OWNER

Attorney Information

```
                              )
                              )     Court Information
                              )
                              )        Case No. _____
                              )
Parties                       )     STOP NOTICE TO OWNER
                              )
_____ )
```

TO: _____

YOU ARE HEREBY NOTIFIED that on the _____day of
_____, 19__ (or between the dates of _____, 19__ and
_____, 19__) I, _____, the undersigned performed (or agreed to perform) labor for you (or furnished or agreed to furnish material to you) at the request of (general contractor or other party) on (or used in the work of improvement or building constructed on the property) located at (give address or legal description) of which you are (reputed) owner.

The following labor (or materials) has (have) been performed (or furnished):
(Here state the labor or materials furnished by the client).

The amount and value of that (already) performed (or already furnished) is
_____ Dollars, and the amount in value of the whole agreed to be performed (orfurnished) is _____ Dollars.

_____(general contractor or the person having authority) promised and agreed to pay the undersigned as follows:

(Here you should set forth the arrangements or the installment payments due or whatever arrangements were made for the man to be paid) but has failed and refused and continues to fail and refuse to pay any part thereof (or if the contractor was paid a certain sum of money then state what he was paid and what the balance is left unpaid that is still due and owing).

Therefore, the undersigned hereby requests and demands that you withhold from said _____ (this would be the general contractor or other person in authority) the sum of _____ Dollars.

DATED: _____       _____
                            Claimant
                            Address

## Complaint for Breach of Contract

It is vitally important that you include in Paragraph I the fictitious name of the plaintiff and that the plaintiff has in fact fulfilled the requirements of the state regulations regarding the certificate and notice being published according to law.

As to Paragraphs III, IV and V, wherein you allege the right of the defendant to operate, you should have checked the Secretary of State or other appropriate agency to determine if the defendant corporation is a corporation in good standing in your state. In this connection, you should also verify that said defendant corporation has the right to operate in your state.

At Paragraph VIII, once again you are cautioned to spell out the legal description of the property involved in your complaint for foreclosure. Failure to do this can subject your complaint to a demurrer or perhaps even a motion to strike.

As you will recall, your first cause of action is for breach of contract, hence, you must set forth under what conditions and what you are alleging is the breach on the part of the defendant, and how the same has been detrimental to the plaintiff. Therefore, your second cause of action would include each paragraph of your first cause of action up to and including damages, and further, would include how the defendant is using the corporation as his or her alter ego. The third cause of action, therefore, would include Paragraphs I through X, or whatever they are of the first cause of action (leaving out the damages clause) and the second cause of action (leaving out the damages clause) and then go forth and set forth the basis upon which you are seeking a foreclosure of a mechanic's lien and recall of bond.

Your prayer, should include what damages you are requesting as to the first cause of action, second cause of action and third cause of action.

*Caution:* Be sure in preparing your causes of action that they are addressed to the proper defendant. This is because, for example, you had listed defendant corporation, a Delaware corporation, John Smith, president of said corporation, and John Smith, individually; Mary Smith, Vice President, Mary Smith, individually, etc. If this is true, then you should spell out in your first, second and third causes of action which defendant is guilty either of the breach, or using the corporation's alter ego, or responsible for bringing this action to a head to the point that your client had to foreclose on the mechanic's lien and bond.

This type of procedure should be followed through in your Prayer. That is to say, consider the following:

> FIRST CAUSE OF ACTION as to all defendants and each of them .....
> SECOND CAUSE OF ACTION as to all defendants and each of them

.....

OR

> SECOND CAUSE OF ACTION as to defendant MARY SMITH, individually, .....

And so on.

Then your last paragraphs would be as to all defendants, and each of them, for costs of suit, etc.

COMPLAINT FOR BREACH OF CONTRACT

Attorneys for Plaintiff

MUNICIPAL COURT OF THE STATE OF _____<br>_____ COUNTY JUDICIAL DISTRICT

|  |  |
|---|---|
| ) | NO. _____ |
| ) | |
| ) | COMPLAINT FOR BREACH OF |
| Plaintiff, ) | CONTRACT, ALTER EGO, |
| ) | FORECLOSURE OF MECHANIC'S |
| vs. ) | LIEN AND ON BOND |
| ) | |
| ) | |
| ) | |
| Defendants. ) | |
| ) | |
| _____ ) | |

Plaintiff alleges:

FIRST CAUSE OF ACTION

I

At all times mentioned herein, Plaintiff, _____, was and now is a corporation duly organized and existing under and by virtue of the laws of the State of _____, and is doing business under the fictitious business name of _____, and has filed the Certificate and published the Notice required by _____ Business and Professions Code Section _____, et seq.

## II

At all times mentioned herein, plaintiff has been and now is a duly licensed, excavating, grading and paving contractor licensed by the State of _____ and authorized to perform all of the works, hereinafter alleged as performed upon the property hereinafter described, in the above-entitled judicial district.

## III

Plaintiff is informed and believes and upon such information and belief, alleges that Defendant, _____, is a corporation organized and existing under and by virtue of the laws of the State of _____.

## IV

Plaintiff is informed and believes and, upon such information and belief, alleges that Defendant, _____, is a _____ corporation, organized and existing under and by virtue of the laws of the State of

_____.

## V

Plaintiff is informed and believes and, upon such information and belief, alleges that Defendant, _____, is a corporation duly authorized to transact a surety business in the State of _____.

## VI

Plaintiff has no information or belief regarding the state of incorporation of the other alleged corporate defendants named herein.

## VII

The true names or capacities, whether individual, corporate, associate, or otherwise, of the Defendants herein named as DOES 1 through 50, inclusive, are unknown to Plaintiff, who therefore sues said Defendants by said fictitious names and Plaintiff requests permission to amend this Complaint to substitute the true names of such Defendants and their capacities when the same have been ascertained.

## VIII

Plaintiff is informed and believes and upon such information and belief alleges that Defendants, _____, and DOES 1 through 25, inclusive, are now and at all times have been owners, or the reputed owners, of that certain parcel of real property located in the City of _____, County of _____, State of _____, more particularly described as follows: ....

## Notice of Filing Lien for Mechanic's Lien ...

A sample of a Notice of Filing Lien for Mechanic's Lien as to trade in Oklahoma is set forth for your review. Note that you should spell out with clarity on whom the Notice is being served with the correct address. This is vital. Serving the wrong person or having the notice delivered to the wrong address could kill your claim and thwart your statutory period. It is for this reason that these notices should be sent by registered mail, return receipt requested.

Note further that in the paragraph regarding the description of real property, you should include the legal description of the property as on the deed or title report received from a title insurance company.

Relative to the contract, please be sure to set forth the exact date of the contract, and who are the parties privy to the contract, as well as the sum agreed upon as between the parties.

## NOTICE OF FILING LIEN FOR MECHANIC'S LIEN

Attorney Information

Court Information

)        Case No. _____
)
)        NOTICE OF FILING LIEN FOR
Parties                    )        MECHANIC'S LIEN ...
)        (_____, _____)
)
)
_____  )

TO: _____
ADDRESS: _____
You are herby notified, that the undersigned _____ of _____, State of _____, did on the _____ day of _____, 19__, file its claim for a Mechanic's Lien and materialman's statements as a subcontractor, in the office of the _____ _____ in and for the County of _____, State of _____, upon and against the following described real property located in the County of, State of _____, to wit:

(Here you should set forth succinctly and completely the description of the real property involved.)

That the undersigned claimant asserts a lien on the property by reason of the _____ contract with one _____ contractor, and this claimant asserts a lien upon the real property in the sum of _____ Dollars by reason thereof, being the balance due this claimant on the account, and this notice is for the purpose of informing you of the filing of the statement and claim for the lien.

_____

CLAIM OF LIEN

Attorney Information

                                      Court Information

                          )    Case No. _____
                          )
                          )
    Parties                )    CLAIM OF LIEN
                          )
                          )    _____
    _____)

    STATE OF _____
                            )  SS
    COUNTY OF _____)

_____(name of lienor), _____ (residence or business address of lienor), being duly sworn, states that pursuant to a contract with _____ (name of lienor's employer or person with whom he contracted) he (performed, furnished) the following (labor and services and materials):

(Here describe the labor or services performed or material furnished in detail. You should describe specifically and specially the fabricated materials separately).

_____ to the value of _____ (Which is the contract price) on the following described real property (describe the real property succinctly and clearly for identification being sure to give the access street and number, if known) owned by _____ (name of owner against whose interest the lien is claimed) whose interest in such real property is (state owner's interest in the property if known).

And further states that the last item of _____ (and that would be labor, services, material, etc.) was (furnished, performed, etc.) on the _____ day of _____, 19__ and of the contract price (here state the amount unpaid) for which amount he claims a lien on the real property described.

                                  _____

                                  Signature of Lienor

Subscribed and sworn to before me this _____ day of _____, 19__.

                                  _____

                                  Signature of Lienor

                                  _____

                                  Notary Public in and for said
                                  County and State

Expiration Date of Commission

# CHAPTER 8

# Working with the Rules of Evidence

*The primary objectives of this chapter are to set forth the form and mode of discovery of evidence; and the role played by the paralegal in obtaining admissible evidence to be used by the attorney at the time of trial.*

## INTRODUCTION

Legal assistants must have a full understanding of the basic rules of evidence to be of service to the attorney insofar as it enables them to develop their evidence through discovery procedures in preparing the attorney's case for trial. To this extent, you should know what rules affect the admissibility or inadmissibility of evidence to be presented to the court for consideration.

## A. Elements of Evidence

1. The information must be relevant to the issues;
2. The information must be something which can be perceived;
3. It must have some reason to prove or disprove a relevant fact;
4. It must be of consequence—not irrelevant;
5. The material must be relevant to the credibility of the issue involved; and
6. It must be useful to the trier of facts in rendering a decision.

## Overcoming Evidential Problems

1. Your tangible admissions of evidence (your documentary evidence or writings), can be self-authenticated (certification of a document), or can be certified by the proper authority;

2. Thereafter, prior to the time of trial, you should gather them all together in one place for the convenience of your attorney;

3. You can have these documents and other writings self-authenticated in the following manner:

   a. By attestation of the clerk of the court, with the seal of the court affixed; or

   b. By the officer in whose custody the record is legally kept under seal of his office;

   c. By a certificate of a chief judge or presiding magistrate of the court, to the effect that the person so attesting the record is a clerk of the court; or that he is the officer in whose custody the record is required by law to be kept; and that his signature to the attestation is genuine; and finally,

   d. By notarization before a duly, licensed notary public.

4. Another way to overcome the tangible admissions of evidence is to have them authenticated. This can be done at or during the trial of the action, wherein the attorney lays the foundation for the introduction of the document and thereafter proceeds to prove that the document is what it is alleged to be. This is purely within the attorney's bailiwick and should be no concern of yours.

5. Another way to overcome tangible admissions of evidence as they relate to demonstrative evidence is to be sure that any experiments or scientific demonstrations, or explanations of charge and grafts, are gathered together in one place for the benefit of the attorney and/or his expert witness.

All evidence and/or opinions which are statements of witnesses fall within The Best Evidence Rule, Parole Evidence Rule and The Hearsay Rule, all of which are within the bailiwick of the attorney and should be of no concern to the legal assistant.

Consider and review the following:

### STATEMENT OF HYPOTHETICAL FACTS

Jane Jones, and baby, were passengers on a train, the Silver Meteor, from Washington, D.C. to Miami, Florida, and were killed by a collision between the Southern Trains, Silver Meteor and Blue Special.

Jane Jones, and baby, purchased First Class tickets from Washington, D.C. on December 28, 1973. The trip was uneventful until the Silver Meteor reached the outskirts of a little town called Vaney, South Carolina, where the collision occurred. Several coaches were derailed, and as a result of the derailment, Jane Jones and baby were crushed to death between the seats of the coach which they were riding.

These are the facts obtained from the husband of the decedent. Your attorney asks you now to prepare a memorandum of law to establish negligence on the part of the defendant. (This is your issue for which you must obtain admissible evidence.) Immediately you know it is a wrongful death action. Further, you know that the burden will be on your attorney to prove that the decedent had a legal right to be on the train, and therefore, you must establish privity of the contract. To do this you must establish prima facie evidence of the purchase of First Class tickets by Jane Jones and baby.

As a result, you would do either of the following:

(a) Secure duplicate copies of the tickets, if they are available or possible;

(b) Secure a copy of the passenger list and have it authenticated by the appropriate officer or agency;

(c) Subpoena copies of said list for copying by way of a deposition or Motion for Production of Documents, or

(d) If the tickets were purchased with a credit card or other similar activity, secure copies of the invoice by way of a Motion for Production of Documents for Inspection and Copying.

Once you have established the decedent's legal right to be on the train, your attorney can show that the defendant violated a duty of care in its negligent operation of an inherently dangerous instrument, i.e., a railroad train.

## SUPPORTING ALLEGATIONS WITH THE WEIGHT OF THE EVIDENCE

Since your job as a legal assistant will be to handle facts of the case and do the legal research to support the theory and statutes for the attorney, we submit the following hypothetical step-by-step procedures in establishing negligence:

You have secured your authenticated documents; now you must develop your legal memorandum in support of negligence on the part of the attorney. In this instance, we will use the doctrine of *Res Ipsa Loquitur,* that is, "the thing speaks for itself." If you intend to rely on this document, you have the burden of producing evidence to establish the following:

A. That the accident occurred and that it was the type of accident which would not have occurred had it not been for the negligence of the defendant. To do this, you must have an on-site investigation to determine if the rails or other equipment were defective; whether the brakes on the train or automobile were defective; needed repair; if the driver was drunk or had he been drinking; if he had poor eyesight; if he wore glasses, and if so, was he wearing them at the time of the collison, and so forth.

B. That the defendant (or agent, servant or employee) had exclusive control of the train or car or other vehicle. To establish this, secure names, addresses and capacity or title of person driving or manning the train or truck at the time of the collision and the immediate supervisor; get copies of payroll sheets and personnel files.

C. That the plaintiff in no way contributed to the accident, either voluntarily or otherwise. Establish this by seeking out survivors of the accident or persons who may have witnessed the plaintiff; who may have talked to her; aided her in some way or were passengers and so forth.

## ESTABLISHING AND PROVING A
## PRIMA FACIE CASE IN REPLEVIN

Since a suit in replevin is a personal, possessory type action, plaintiff must recover on the strength of his title in the property and not on the weakness of the defendant's title. Plaintiff must establish his right to possession of the property prior to the commencement of the action. For this reason, your interview with the client should set forth succinctly the following:

1. Prima Facie evidence of title;

2. Ownership and conversion by the defendant which would be an outright act. As a result of this interview, a lawsuit for conversion and return of personal property; or in the alternative, for a money judgment equivalent to the prevailing price, should be filed.

## Step-by-Step Procedure

If, thereafter, the case goes to trial and a judgment is received, money or return of property is ordered, you should do the following:

1. Obtain an abstract of judgment, have it certified and file it in the county where the property is located;

2. Secure a Writ of Execution from the court;

3. Forward the Writ to the appropriate marshal or sheriff's office for execution of the judgment.

(Check your local state and court rules to determine the time restriction in connection with this procedure).

## ESTABLISHING PRIMA FACIE EVIDENCE ON AN INSURANCE POLICY CLAIM

1. You must establish that the policy in dispute was issued upon the life of the decedent.

2. That he was the owner of said policy BEFORE HIS DEATH.

3. That the policy is within the possession of the plaintiff with the name thereon of the insured and the deceased being the same.

If, for whatever reason, the plaintiff or your client does not have the policy in his possession, you can do the following:

A. Send out a set of special interrogatories to the insurance agent issuing the policy with the request for attachments, i.e., a certified copy of policy and/or original application;

B. Set up a deposition, with subpoena duces tecum, requesting that the insurance agent bring with him the policy and the application or certified copies thereof for copying.

In connection with proof of death, if the same is denied as not having been received by the insurance company, a notice to produce should be served before the date of trial, and if the defendant fails to produce such notice and proof of death, secondary evidence will have to be introduced.

You, as the legal assistant, have the responsibility, therefore, of being sure that the client has notified the insurance company and complied with all necessary and prerequisite steps to secure payment of the insurance policy. If you find that the plaintiff has complied with all of the steps, then draft and file the notice to produce as indicated above.

Prior to trial, the notice should be served on opposing counsel, describing in detail the written instrument to be produced at trial, and state thereon that in the event of his failure to do so, secondary evidence will be offered. This notice should be sent out at least ten days (or whatever statutory limitation is required in your state) prior to the date of trial. Thereafter, if opposing counsel fails to produce, plaintiff can then present the notice to produce with proof of service as evidence.

## UNLAWFUL DETAINER ACTION

The rule of law is that a tenant cannot, without the prior written consent of the landlord, create a new tenancy by holding over after the expiration of a lease. Prima facie evidence to establish this right can be found in your local state codes.

### Step-by-Step

Once you have checked your statutory requirements, do the following:

1. As a first step to get the defendant out of the premises, prepare and have personally served upon said defendant a notice to quit (3-day, 10-day or 30-day notice depending on what is required by the plaintiff and according to statutory regulations).

2. If, after said notice, your client advises that defendant is still in the premises, then file a complaint for unlawful detainer.

3. *Caution:* We have found it expedient to have all documents prepared at the time the notice to quit is prepared and served. This avoids the last-minute rush to get the documents prepared and filed with the court before the running of the statute. Your attorney will appreciate this extra effort and it will save you a lot of time and wracked nerves.

4. In most states, the defendant will have ten days in which to answer a complaint for unlawful detainer, some states now make it 30 days. In any event, the default procedure or preparation for trial thereafter is the same as with any other litigation.

## ESTABLISHING A PRIMA FACIE CASE
## IN A CONTRACT CLAIM

1. Secure duplicates of the contract, if available or possible; or

2. Secure a copy and have it authenticated by the appropriate officer or individual; or

3. Subpoena copies for copying by way of a deposition; or

4. Notice a motion for production of documents; and/or

5. Obtain a witness who can testify to the contents of the contract or the fact that the contract was signed in his or her presence.

UNLAWFUL DETAINER COMPLAINT

Attorney for Plaintiffs

COUNTY MUNICIPAL COURT
STATE OF _____

|  |  |  |
|---|---|---|
| | ) | No. _____ |
| | ) | |
| Plaintiffs, | ) | C O M P L A I N T |
| | ) | FOR UNLAWFUL DETAINER |
| | ) | AND RENT |
| vs. | ) | |
| | ) | |
| | ) | |
| | ) | |
| Defendant. | ) | |
| | ) | |
| _____ | ) | |

Plaintiffs allege:

I

_____, a _____ corporation, is now and at all times herein mentioned was a corporation organized and existing under and by virtue of the laws of the State of _____, and authorized to do business and engage in business in the State of _____ with its offices located at _____.

II

_____, a New
Jersey corporation, is now and at all times herein mentioned as a corporation
organized and existing under and by virtue of the laws of the State of New Jersey,
and authorized to do business and engage in business in the State of
_____ with its offices located at

III

Plaintiffs, and each of them, are now and at all times herein mentioned, were
and now are co-partners doing business under the fictitious firm name and style of
_____, and have filed the Certificate and published notice as required
by Civil Code 2466 and 2468.

IV

The Plaintiffs are the Owners of the premises located at _____
and are entitled to possession of the same.

V

On February 15, 19___, Plaintiffs, and each of them, rented said premises
to-wit: _____, at a rental of One Hundred Ninety-Five Dollars ($195)
per month, pursuant to a Lease Agreement, a copy of which is attached hereto and
marked Exhibit "A", the terms of which are incorporated herein by reference as
though fully set forth herein.

VI

Defendant has been in possession of said premises ever since February 15,
19__, and has continued to occupy same to the present.

VII

During the period from October 15, 19__ to present, Defendant is in default
of rent, accruing to date of Notice to Pay Rent or Quit in the amount of One
Hundred Ninety-Five Dollars ($195).

VIII

On October 23, 19__, Plaintiffs caused to be served on Defendant (Declaration of Service attached hereto and marked Exhibit "B" and incorporated herein as
though fully set forth) a written Notice to Pay Rent or Deliver Up Possession of the
Premises within (3) three days after service of said Notice (a copy of which is
attached hereto and marked Exhibit "C" and incorporated herein as though fully
set forth).

IX

More than three (3) days have elapsed since the service of said Notice on
Defendant but no part of said defaulted rent has been paid, and Defendant willfully
continues in unlawful possession of said premises without consent of the Plaintiffs.

X

The rental value of said premises is $195 per month or $6.50 per day. Plaintiffs are sustaining damages by reason of said unlawful detainer and detention of said premises in said sum each day commencing October 15, 19___.

WHEREFORE, Plaintiffs pray judgment against the Defendant as follows:

1. Restitution of said premises;

2. Rent due for the period from October 15, 19___ to present in the amount of $195 and for such further rental as may accrue from the time of the filing of this complaint to the rendition of judgment herein;

3. Damages for the unlawful withholding of the possession of said premises subsequent to the expiration of three (3) days after service of notice, and for TREBLE said sum as provided by statute; and for declaration that said Lease and agreement be forfeited;

4. For reasonable attorneys' fees;

5. For costs of suit incurred herein;

6. For such other and further relief as the Court deem just.

Dated: November 4, 19___.

_____

Attorney for Plaintiff

## COMPLAINT FOR SPECIFIC PERFORMANCE
## OF CONTRACT TO CONVEY LAND
(As prepared under Federal Rules of Civil Procedure
and Federal Rules of Evidence)

1. Allegation of jurisdiction.

2. On or about December 1, 19___, plaintiff and defendant entered into an agreement in writing, a copy of which is attached hereto as Exhibit "A".

3. In accordance with the provisions of said agreement, plaintiff tendered to defendant the purchase price and requested a conveyance of the land, but defendant refused to accept the tender and refused to make conveyance.

4. Plaintiff now offers to pay the purchase price.

WHEREFORE, plaintiff demands:

1. That defendant be required to specifically perform said agreement;

2. That damages in the sum of _____ dollars be awarded;

3. That if specific performance is not granted, plaintiff have judgment against the defendant in the sum of _____ dollars; ....

_____

Signature

# Casualty Claims

*A casualty claim, for the most part, is based on a tort—a wrong committed by a defendant against a plaintiff, for which plaintiff can file a valid cause of action based on defendant's negligence. This chapter gives you the knowledge to make this determination.*

# CHAPTER 9

## INTRODUCTION

Casualty claims (torts) for the most part, are based upon the violation of a duty owned to another which results in injury to the person or to property. Though this type of tort is not dependent upon a contractual relationship between parties, it does give rise to a legal cause of action. The existence of a duty imposed by law and a violation of that duty are the necessary elements to establish a prima facie case for negligence.

IN A NUTSHELL:

A valid cause of action based on negligence should include the following which must be present in order for you to have prepared a prima facie cause of action:

1. A duty owed;
2. A breach of that duty;
3. Actual and proximate cause as it relates to the breach of duty; and
4. Injury or damages caused by the breach of a duty.

## DOCTRINES AFFECTING LIABILITY

Remember, when preparing your complaint and in interviewing the client, that it must be determined at the initial stage what doctrine affects the liability of the parties involved. To this end, consider the following:

A. The *Prudent Man Test* which is commonly used in common law cases and may still be used in some jurisdictions.

B. The doctrine of *Res Ipsa Loquitur* which is commonly called the "But for" test, and states in essence that "But for the negligent act of defendant, the accident would not have occurred." To apply this doctrine, the following elements must be overt and measurable:

    (i) That the accident could not have occurred unless someone was negligent;

    (ii) That the nature of the negligence must be within the scope of a duty that is owed to the plaintiff; and

    (iii) That the defendant did absolutely nothing to contribute to the accident.

C. Then you have the doctrine of *Last Clear Chance*. This doctrine stands for the proposition that the contributory negligence of the plaintiff will not prevent his recovery, if it appears that the defendant, by the exercise of reasonable care and prudence, had the last clear chance to avoid the accident.

FOR EXAMPLE:

In a three-car accident, your client was alert enough to see Driver #1 run through a red light and crash into a car making a left turn. To avoid hitting Car #2, he quickly changed lanes. This is a hypothesis which sets up the "last clear chance" to avoid an accident

D. The doctrine of *Negligence per se* varies from jurisdiction to jurisdiction since it is based on state statute and the negligent act is compounded by a violation of that state law from its inception.

FOR EXAMPLE:

Say Mary was driving in excess of the legal speed, and in so doing ran a red light, hitting a pedestrian, who was crossing the street with a green light, in the crosswalk.

In this instance, Mary violated the following statutes designed to protect the pedestrian:

    (i) Driving in excess of the speed limit set by law;

    (ii) Running through a red light in violation of the law; and

    (iii) Hitting an innocent bystander, the pedestrian.

## LIABILITY OF THE PARTIES DETERMINED

Inasmuch as it would be your responsibility to draft complaints from scratch, recall the various denominators upon which you can base your complaint.

Recall the following well-established causal connections between plaintiff and defendant:

1) *Proximate cause.* Proximate cause is the primary cause of an injury or damage which is established by showing that it was not only the natural, but also the probable consequence of the negligent act, i.e., Mary running the red light.

2) *Intervening cause.* The intervening cause is the material cause in determining legal causation of the injury to the plaintiff. It must supersede the prior wrongful act. It is an unforeseeable, independent act which destroys the causal connection between the negligent acts of the defendants and the wrongful injuries. For example, the criminal act of a third party which causes injury not intended or foreseeable by the defendant.

Or, Mary being put in sudden danger of her life or limbs by the negligent act of Sue, instinctively attempting to escape such injury, and in so doing causes injury to herself or to bystanders.

3) *Concurrent causes.* Concurrent causes are the negligent acts of two persons, occurring at the same time where the accident would not have happened absent the negligence of either party. In this instance, both parties are liable, and the acts of both are deemed to be the proximate cause of the accident.

## WHAT ARE THE DEFENSES TO THESE LIABILITIES?

You are cautioned to check your local statutes as to their applicability in your state before utilizing them in preparing your complaint.

1) *Contributory Negligence.* This is a defense to an action based upon the negligence of plaintiff as set forth above.

2) *Comparative Negligence.* This determines the degree of liability of the plaintiff and how much he may recover based upon his contribution to the accident or injury.

3) *Imputed Negligence.* This doctrine is applied to defeat the liability to the plaintiff by charging him with concurrent negligence of a bystander; or to defeat a negligence action by imputing to plaintiff the contributory negligence of a third party.

> *Note:* This doctrine is normally used in an agency relationship, such as master/servant; parties to a joint enterprise, etc.

4) *Assumption of the Risk.* Under this doctrine the plaintiff must have known and understood the danger and assumed the risk of that danger voluntarily.

FOR EXAMPLE:

The risk of death in going over Niagara Falls in a barrel when you cannot swim; or the danger of slipping on ice when you do not know how to skate; or breaking a leg skiing down a slope when you do not know how to ski, and so forth.

## OTHER LIABILITIES YOU SHOULD BE AWARE OF

1) *Strict Liability*. This liability is applicable where there is no blame on either the plaintiff's or defendant's part, and as such the court must decide who should suffer the consequences of any resulting injuries or other damages. A common case where the doctrine of strict liability is used is in the ownership of animals. It is used when the animal has a tendency to act in such a way that is likely to cause injury to others.

FOR EXAMPLE:

A big dog jumping up on individuals can be considered vicious and dangerous. This tendency, if the animal is domesticated, would have to be proved; but in the case of a wild animal, the courts tend to presume that the animal is vicious and dangerous.

FOR EXAMPLE:

Say you own a German shepherd who is a guard dog, and you keep him locked up most of the time, but he gets out of the house while you are away and injures your next door neighbor. This would be the basis of a simple negligence case and the plaintiff could recover for any damages sustained.

Another area where the doctrine of strict liability is used is that of the ultra-hazardous activity. Under this doctrine, liability is established as follows:

    (a) The escape of dangerous substances brought onto the land;
    (b) An improper use of land; and
    (c) Misuse of water.

Examples of these ultra-hazardous activities are:

    (a)  Dynamite blastings;
    (b)  Oil drillings; and
    (c)  Spraying crops with insecticide.

2) *Products Liability*. In developing a case based on products liability, include the following:

- (a) The manufacturer has placed the product on the market;
- (b) The manufacturer knew that the product would be used without inspection for defects;
- (c) The product was defective and caused injury or damage to plaintiff;
- (d) The plaintiff used the product in the way and manner for which it was intended.

## DEFENSES TO A PRODUCTS LIABILITY CASE

1) As a general rule, contributory negligence on the part of the plaintiff is not a defense to a products liability action.

2) A plaintiff may be barred from recovery on the ground of assumption of risk.

3) Unreasonable use of the product; or using it in a manner for which it was not intended.

## CHECKLIST FOR THE PARAPROFESSIONAL WORKING WITH A CASUALTY CLAIM OR TORT ACTION

Before commencing to draft your complaint, check the following:

A. Is there in fact a cause of action, i.e., was there duty owed? If so, was there a violation of that duty; were there damages sustained as a result of the alleged breach or violation of the duty owed?

If there is no cause of action in fact supported by the allegations, the complaint will fail. This being true, a demurrer (general or special) can be filed; or you can move to dismiss the action.

B. If there was a duty, determine the nature of the duty of care owed or required under the circumstances, such as, ordinary care, specialized, and the like. This affects the damages allowable or which can be prayed for and sustained.

C. As to causation, determine if the incident was the proximate cause, actual or intervening cause of the breach, harm, or other resulting damage. This procedure aids you in determining whether or not the proper parties or all of the parties have been joined and made a party to this action.

D. As to damages:

(1) Determine the nature of the liability involved such as whether it was strict liability, products liability, and so forth;

(2) Determine the nature of the negligence, if applicable, such as negligence per se, contributory negligence, comparative negligence, assumption of a risk, etc. The purpose of this determination is to ascertain the extent, if any, of the client's responsibility, which of course, could and would mitigate the liability of the defendant.

E. Determine what affirmative defenses (or cross-complaint) can be filed or alleged. This is to offset the liability of the client; or to dismiss the complaint of the plaintiff.

F. And, of course, check the statute of limitations problem—if applicable.

All of the above items should be reviewed by you prior to drafting the complaint in any tort action, including a medical malpractice lawsuit.

## THE MEDICAL MALPRACTICE DEFENSE

As it relates to a medical malpractice lawsuit, all of the above and foregoing should, of course, be considered. In addition, check the following:

1. The standard of care allotted to a physician, as:

(i) The degree of his learning skills;

(ii) His use of ordinary care and diligence in applying his learning and skills.

### Establishing Violations of the Above Duties

Note that in many jurisdictions the courts have spelled out what constitutes a violation of a physician's duty, such as:

(a) A physician may be considered negligent if he fails to hospitalize a patient when the standard of care indicates hospitlization is necessary.

(b) A physician may be considered to be in violation of his duty of care by his lack of diligence in attending to his patient.

(c) A physician may be considered in violation of his duty of care if he unjustifiably abandons or neglects his patient after sufficient notice, excuse or mutual agreement.

(d) A physician may be considered to be in violation of his duty of care if he promises results which are not forthcoming, as the results of a treatment prescribed or surgery performed.

(e) A physician may be considered to be in violation of his duty of care if he fails to explain or inform the patient as to the nature of proposed surgery, and if he fails to obtain an informed, intelligent consent to said surgery. (The exception to this rule, in some jurisdictions, is emergency surgery.)

> *Caution:* A plaintiff has no medical malpractice case unless he can establish that one or more of the above were omitted or occurred; and that the same was the proximate cause of the injury or death of a patient.

## Legal Doctrines Affecting Medical Malpractice

A. *Res Ipsa Loquitur.* This is the presumption of negligence on the part of the physician. The physician must show:

   (a) A satisfactory explanation of the incident;
   (b) That some unpresentable cause precipitated the injury despite his exercise of care.

B. *Respondent Superior.* Here, the physician is not responsible for procedures or conduct of hospital physicians or nurses performed or carried out *independently,* and not under his exclusive control, unless he was negligent in the choice of his supporting staff.

C. *Statute of Limitations.* Though the statutory time restriction varies from state to state, in California it is basically a 5-year statute of limitations period.

FOR EXAMPLE:

If you have surgery of whatever nature, you have four years within which to discover negligence; and one year from the date of such discovery within which to file a complaint for medical malpractice.

The date of the injury, illness, or disability proximately caused by the malpractice is a key factor.)

FOR EXAMPLE:

If some foreign object was left in the body of a patient by the physician, the statute of limitations would begin to run when it is discovered that a foreign object is lodged in the body.

(Note that any material concealment or misrepresentation by the physician tolls the statute of limitations until the patient discovers or reasonably should have discovered the facts.)

## Step-by-Step Procedure in Defending a Medical Malpractice Lawsuit

1) When a complaint is received in your office, your attorney will tell you how he thinks it should be answered. You should, however, review the complaint yourself to determine if he has overlooked anything.

FOR EXAMPLE:

A possible demurrer to a request for punitive damages. Should you discover this, advise your attorney and obtain permission to file a special demurrer to this allegation.

2) Or, the attorney may have noted on the complaint to go forward and file an answer alleging affirmative defenses.

FOR EXAMPLE:

A "good samaritan" defense; or contributory negligence.

EXAMPLE OF AN ANSWER:

"If in fact plaintiff sustained any injury and damages of any nature whatsoever by reason of anything done, or omitted to be done by the defendant, which fact is not admitted, but is merely stated for the purpose of this defense, said injury and damage, if any, was approximately caused by the negligence of the plaintiff in failing to take proper and reasonable measure for their (his, her) own well-being."

*Note:* It is vitally important in this type of lawsuit to include affirmative defenses. Therefore, if your attorney, for whatever reason, overlooked to instruct you to allege affirmative defenses, do it anyway; or bring this oversight to his attention.

3) Thereafter, or concurrently therewith, prepare and cause to be filed a set of interrogatories and request for admissions directed to the plaintiff.

### TRIED AND PROVEN MEASURE:

It is suggested that you mark these documents ''First Set of Interrogatories,'' since it has been our experience in these types of lawsuits that more than one set of interrogatories and request for admissions are required to obtain the necessary information needed and wanted by your attorney.

4) Often you will find that you have to compel answers to the interrogatories or request for admissions, and since you are defending the action, immediately upon the expiration of the statutory time within which plaintiff has to file an answer, prepare a motion to compel answers or further answers.

5) As it relates to your duty in answering the interrogatories served on the doctor, be sure to meticulously scrutinize, review and edit, and in some instances, rewrite the answers submitted by the doctor. One major factor you should look for is the name(s) of other doctors and nurses who may have worked with the patient; or perhaps may have been involved in the surgical procedure, to determine if there is any possible conflict of interests, such as your office representing him as general counsel or otherwise.

6) Check to see if in the interrogatories there was a request for information as to the finances of the doctor. If so, check the complaint to see if there was an allegation for punitive damages. If punitive damages were not pleaded, or were pleaded incorrectly, then the doctor does not have to answer the interrogatory since the request for punitive damages will not stand.

If, initially, you have filed a demurrer to the allegation regarding punitive damages, and the demurrer was overruled, this will allow the allegation on punitive damages to stand, which has the effect of allowing plaintiff to inquire into the financial status of a doctor. This being true, the doctor would then have to answer the interrogatory.

7) Obtain copies of any and all medical reports in the possession or under the control of the patient for your attorney, and the insurance company (get copies from your doctor also for comparison).

All other things being equal, the step-by-step procedure for medical malpractice lawsuits is the same as any other lawsuit, such as taking depositions, trial setting conferences, mandatory settlement conferences, and the like. It is important that you include the doctor in all of your conferences.

## FILING A CLAIM AGAINST A MUNICIPALITY
## OR OTHER LEGAL ENTITY

### Practical Step-by-Step Procedure

1. File the Claim, which is normally a printed form secured from the municipality or entity.

2. (Or, if the client is late in obtaining the services of your attorney, then obtain an Application for Leave to Present a Late Claim.)

3. This latter document should be accompanied by a Notice of Petition for Relief from governmental restrictions and an Order that suit may be filed.

4. Prepare a Declaration in support of your Petition, attaching a copy of the proposed Claim thereto.

5. If the Petition is approved, prepare the Order, file the original and copies with the appropriate court clerk, serve a copy on the Board of Supervisors (or other comparable board in your state). If the Board does not object, the judge will sign the original Order and return a conformed copy to your offices.

6. Note on your calendar that you will have thirty (30) days from receipt of this signed Order in which to file your Complaint.

## WORKING WITH A PERSONAL INJURY-
## PROPERTY DAMAGE ACTION

### How to Handle a Complaint

When a complaint comes in to the office you should immediately do the following:

1. Set up a file and index card, and if applicable, obtain an extension of time within which to answer. Calendar the same on your follow-up desk calendar or master calendar, and then place in the appropriate docket book.

2. Examine the complaint to determine if a routine answer, general denial, or affirmative defense is needed.

3. Examine the proof of service to determine if proper service was made, and if not, whether you can file a motion to strike or special

demurrer or other similar type document. (It is advised that you check with your attorney in connection with this procedure.)

4. If you find that you can file a simple answer, then draft such a document and attach it to the file and place it on your attorney's desk.

5. If the complaint has more than one cause of action, we have found it best to determine under what theory the complaint should be drawn, such as common count, alter ego, breach of contract, negligence, etc. This will aid you in stating your affirmative defenses.

### FOR EXAMPLE:

Plaintiff's first cause of action is based on an alleged breach of contract, the second is based on alleged fraud, and the third on alleged acts of conversion.

### PRACTICAL HINT:

A useful personal practice is to put notations of proposed answers in the margin of the complaint/pleading, next to each paragraph, such as the following:

> (Margin)
> Deny      Paragraph 5
> Admit     Paragraph 6

This type of notation makes it easier for your employer to review your work and make any additions, embellishments or suggestions for your final draft.

Thereafter, discuss the routine follow-up steps, such as the schedule for sending out interrogatories, setting up depositions, developing request for admissions, and the need or desire for a jury trial.

6. When a set of interrogatories comes in, review it by comparing the answers, studying the evasions and incomplete responses. Flag them for your attorney for future discussions. This is because your attorney may want to object to some of the interrogatories.

7. At this point you might request from your attorney the feasibility of marshalling requests for admissions. These admissions should be based upon the plaintiff's answers to your interrogatories (or defendant's); statements of witnesses, or their testimony at a deposition or information obtained as a result of a motion to produce documents.

8. If No. 7 is implemented and the plaintiff (defendant) fails to admit certain requests, then an order should be prepared to force the plaintiff (defendant) to admit the same. If this is done, and the plaintiff

(defendant) is allowed to file a response to this motion, then:

9. Review the responses of plaintiff (defendant), to determine the need to request more admissions, and thereafter report your finding to your attorney. This, because at this point, a motion for summary judgment may be in order. If not, you are at-issue.

10. If it is not already prepared, prepare and file an at-issue memorandum with the court (or such other applicable similar document). In most states, this is a printed form and does not have to be signed by opposing counsel, but is merely mailed to him to place him on notice.

11. As a general proposition it takes 3 to 4 weeks before the court sends out a document which may be entitled ''Certificate of Eligibility to File Certificate of Readiness,'' (this may be called something else in your state). This document is the court's way of advising all parties to the action that the case is now on the active civil list, and that the parties may now obtain a trial date.

12. The next step in this procedure would be filing of a court document which could be either a printed form or one from scratch, depending on the policy of your office, and may be called a ''Certificate of Readiness'' or such other applicable name as is used in your state.

FOR EXAMPLE:

In California it is just the opposite of an At-Issue Memorandum, in that this document, the Certificate of Readiness, would have to be signed by both attorneys.

Hence, once you have prepared this ''Certificate of Readiness'' it should be signed by either the defendant or plaintiff attorney, whomever you are representing. Thereafter, once it has been mailed, you should calendar it for return to your office for filing with the court. (In California it is 20 days.) Failing receipt of the return of such completed executed certificate of readiness, the next procedure would be to file an affidavit with the court, setting forth the facts that the other attorney has not returned the executed certificate of readiness to your office for filing in a timely manner. This would force the court to automatically set the case for trial with or without the consent of opposing counsel.

13. After the accomplishment of the foregoing, the court would send out a document with a date of trial and/or a date of settlement

conference, and/or a date of mandatory settlement—whichever is applicable in your state. Your duty in this regard, after the receipt of this document, would be to prepare a notice of trial, notifying the plaintiff of the trial date, and as a courtesy, a notice advising the opposing counsel of said trial date.

14.  You should thereafter, of course, notify the client of the trial date, the settlement conference date, and/or mandatory settlement conference date by letter. We have found it to be the better part of valor to send such a letter by registered mail. This negates the client's saying they had no notice of the trial date and therefore did not appear.

15.  Notify all potential witnesses of the trial date.

*Suggestion:*  Send out a copy of the letter to be returned to you, confirming their appearance at the trial and possible office conference prior to the date of trial to review the facts of the case.

16.  Trial preparation run-down:

(a)  Review the file and determine what witnesses are to be subpoenaed;

(b)  Prepare the subpoenas and hold them in the file until needed;

(c)  Marshal all trial documents, photos, exhibits, and put them in order;

(d)  Start your trial brief (or trial issue brief);

(e)  Draft proposed jury instructions;

(f)  Draft appropriate possible motions that may be needed during the trial or at the end of trial, including notice of appeal; and

(g)  Draft closing documents, arguments, etc.

# Working with a Family Law Matter

*One of the prime duties of a legal assistant in this area of the law is to obtain all necessary facts relating to the assets and rights of the parties. So know the difference, therefore, between community and separate property and how they interact and change their character before preparing your documents.*

**CHAPTER 10**

## CHECKLISTS IN WORKING WITH
## FAMILY LAW MATTERS

### Introduction

One of your prime duties in a law office with a family law practice is that of interviewing the clients, obtaining the necessary facts, and gathering all the information relating to the **property** of the parties. It is a vital function since, from the information you gather, your attorney will be able to analyze what marital state was created and what is the separate, personal property of the parties, as opposed to the community property. The purpose of this chapter is to set forth succinctly the various steps which can be taken in handling either pre-marital documents or those required documents utilized in satisfying the divorce arrangement as between the parties litigant.

### Preparing the Ante-Nuptial Agreement

As you know, this is an agreement between a husband and a wife which is prepared before marriage, but in contemplation of marriage, regarding separate personal property. In order for this agreement to be valid, it must contain the following:

1. A complete disclosure of all separate property of a party; and

2. There must be representation of each party by an attorney of their choosing.

## Alimony and Child Support:

As a general proposition, a court can issue the following orders in connection with alimony and child support:

1. Order for support and maintenance; alimony (if not waived);
2. Order to child custody;
3. Order re visitation rights of the parties;
4. Order for attorney's fees and costs; and
5. Injunctive or restraining order.

## Enforcing Support Orders:

As a guide only, hereinafter set forth are the two methods used in California to enforce the above orders of the court:

A. *Civil Method*

(i) This could be a contempt order or modification order in which a declaration is made as to the amount of the arrearage, the amount ordered to be paid and when; and the balance due. If a modification, then a statement should be included setting forth a change in circumstances, requiring a reduction in the payments.

(ii) This document is filed with the court and the failure of compliance on the part of respondent (or defendant) would result in a money judgment being entered upon which a Writ of Execution could be obtained.

(iii) The Writ of Execution is then delivered to the levying officer on the property of the respondent )or defendant) such as the bank where he keeps his bank account, his automobile, or his place of employment to execute on his salary.

(iv) The proceeds thereafter are physical, taken from the bank; or the levying officer will take the car, etc., in satisfaction of the money judgment for back support payments.

(The above procedure may be followed to collect attorney's fees, alimony payments and child support.)

B. *Criminal Method*

This procedure is used when a party is in contempt of a court order for which he can be imprisoned. However, there must be a hearing to determine his violation and disobedience of the court order. It is a quasi-criminal proceeding, and defendant has to be personally served and physically be present at the hearing though he need not take the stand to testify.

At the time of his hearing, you should prepare an affidavit which sets forth that the defendant had knowledge of the order, either by being in court on the day it was decreed, or had been personally served with a true copy of said order; it should also include that he has the ability to comply with the order; and, that he wilfully disobeyed the court's order at the time he had the ability to pay.

## CHECKLIST FOR DETERMINING SOURCE OF COMMUNITY PROPERTY[1]

The·two common sources of community property are:

A. Earnings during marriage; and

B. Gifts received from third parties.

The earnings during the marriage of the parties are the community property of both, and the gifts received from third parties are personal property of either husband or wife.

*Types of Earnings:*

1. Pension Plans;
2. Apportionment of Insurance Proceeds;
3. Gifts, Bequests, Devisees and Inheritance;
4. Damages—(money from personal injury cases);
5. Credit Acquisitions;
6. Rents, Issues and Profits.

---

[1] Note that there are only about 6 or 7 states out of the 50 states which are "community property" states. The balance are common law states. Thus, this checklist would be applicable only in those states which are governed by "common law" practice and procedure. Check your state statutes for applicable "property" law.

## CHECKLIST FOR COMPLETING
## FAMILY LAW FORMS[2]
## (As Used in California)

### 1. Summons (Marriage)

Do not make the fatal mistake of using the wrong Summons when filing a divorce package. Check to be sure that the Summons is entitled, "Summons re Marriage," or other similar reference to the divorce proceeding. This, because Civil Summonses and "Marriage" Summonses are alike on the face of it.

### 2. Petition (Marriage)

Here again, check your Civil Code Section relating to family law matters to be certain that you have checked the appropriate box marked on the form. Failure to check the appropriate box (or checking the wrong box) can prevent the entry of a default; or, the obtaining of a legal separation, or, the actual dissolution of marriage.

And further, be sure that you have completed all the necessary statistical information needed for identification.

And, moreover, check and double-check to be sure that where required on all documents, the petitioner or respondent has signed the forms applicable.

If necessary and available, include all the attachments which have been referred to in the Petition, such as description of real property, inventory of household furniture and furnishings, list of stocks, and so forth.

THE FOLLOWING MAY NOT BE APPLICABLE IN YOUR STATE; CHECK YOUR COURT RULES FOR THESE PROCEDURES:

### 3. Confidential Questionnaire

In preparing your client's Confidential Questionnaire, be sure you have checked the appropriate box or have spelled out in some manner whose Confidential Questionnaire it is, i.e., petitioner or respondent.

---

[2] In California marriage dissolution and other family law matters are somewhat standarized through the use of official court forms. This is not the case in most states. You should therefore check your local court rules for this procedure since they vary from state to state.

## 4. Confidential Conciliation Statement

The same caution should be used in completing this document as is outlined in No. 3 above. This document is used where the petitioner (or respondent) feels that there is a possibility of reconciling the marriage.

## 5. Financial Declaration

The Financial Declaration also is a vital document, since it advises the court of the financial condition of both parties, and thereby aids the court in making a ruling as to who pays what to whom and when.

BE SURE IT IS COMPLETED CORRECTLY—AND THAT IT IS AS CURRENT AS POSSIBLE.

*Note*: The attorney and the client must sign this document.

## 6. Response (Marriage)

When serving a copy of the divorce papers upon the respondent, be sure that the respondent is served with all documents as required by law, i.e., Summons, Complaint (Petition re Marriage); a blank copy of the Confidential Questionnaire; blank copies of the responsive pleading; Financial Declaration; and if applicable, Order to Show Cause.

In connection with the above, be sure that you check to see if the process server has completed the section of the Proof of Service (normally on the reverse side of the original Summons) correctly, i.e., name of person served, the document served, the date served, and that the Affidavit of Service has been properly dated and signed.

## 7. Notices and Orders to Show Cause

These Notices/Motions and Orders to Show Cause re Contempt, Modification, and so forth, should be prepared meticulously and as a result of conferences with your attorney. In this connection, be sure you check your local rule applicable to the service of the aforementioned documents.

## 8. Request or Declaration re Default (Marriage)

1. Check to determine if a current Financial Declaration is of record; if not, attach a carbon copy to your Request for Default;

2. A copy of this Request or Declaration should be mailed to the last known address of the respondent.

YOU CANNOT SHOW "UNKNOWN" as it relates to the address of a respondent.

## 9. Prepare Your Attorney for Trial

1. Submit the required number of copies of the Interlocutory Judgment of Dissolution (re Marriage) which you have prepared beforehand;

2. Submit the required copies of any Property Settlement Agreement, as well as the original, for filing with the court, if applicable in your state; and

3. Submit the Notice of Entry of Judgment re Marriage.

TACTICAL MEASURE:

Naturally, if it is a full-blown trial, then all documents normally prepared and included for a trial would be applicable here.

The originals of the documents referred to Paragraph 1 through 3 above, ought to be left with the court clerk for processing, and copies of same mailed to all parties-litigants.

## FUNCTIONAL DUTIES OF A LEGAL ASSISTANT
## WORKING WITH A FAMILY LAW PROBLEM[3]

1. Collect and organize data needed for legal actions in domestic relations.
2. Write draft of Petition for Dissolution of Marriage.
3. Write draft of Petition for Separation of Bed and Board.
4. Write Petition of Annulment.
5. Write legally correct Summons to appear in court.
6. Collect data for respondent's Answer to a Petition.
7. Write respondent's Answer to a Petition.
8. Collect data for Petition for Order to Show Cause.
9. Prepare Petition for Order to Show Cause.
10. Collect data to write Order to Show Cause.

---

[3] Source: Oregon Department of Education Curriculum Development Unit Career & Vocational Education.

11. Write draft of citation.
12. Compile and write Order to Show Cause.
13. Collect data needed to prepare Restraining Order.
14. Write legally correct Restraining Order.
15. Collect data for Property Settlement Agreement.
16. Write Agreement on property settlement.
17. Fill out correct record of dissolution.
18. Collect data needed for Affidavit of Non-Military Service.
19. Fill out Affidavit of Non-Military Service.
20. Assemble data needed for Order of Default.
21. Write Order of Default.
22. Prepare Motion and Affidavit for Decree Without Application.
23. Assemble data to prepare Decree of Dissolution of Marriage.
24. Prepare Decree of Dissolution of Marriage.
25. Assemble data to prepare Property Settlement Agreement.
26. Prepare Property Settlement Agreement.
27. Compile Petition for Order to Show Cause Regarding Contempt.
28. Write Court Order to Show Cause Regarding Contempt.
29. Compile Petition to Modify Child Support.
30. Write Petition to Modify Child Support.
31. Write Court Order to Modify Child Support.
32. Collect data for Petition to Change Custody.
33. Write Petition to Change Custody.
34. Write Court Order to Change Custody.
35. Prepare Final Decree of Divorce.

As you know, in some states the filing of a Petition for Dissolution of Marriage is merely a printed form and in other states it is drawn from scratch. To this end, consider the following examples of a Petition for Dissolution of Marriage drawn from scratch, noting that there is apparently no requirement for the code section applicable to be set forth on said Petition.

Also following is a sample of a responsive pleading prepared to be filed on behalf of the respondent in a family law matter. Annotations on this form are self-explanatory.

## PETITION FOR DISSOLUTION OF MARRIAGE

STATE OF _____ )
              ) SS:
COUNTY OF _____ )

IN THE _____ COUNTY
SUPERIOR COURT
CAUSE NO.        ROOM NO.

IN RE:  THE MARRIAGE OF _____

### PETITION FOR DISSOLUTION OF MARRIAGE

Comes now the petitioner, _____, and alleges and says:

1.  That petitioner has been a continuous and bona fide resident of the State of _____ and the County of _____ for more than six (6) months, that the respondent, _____, is a resident of the State of _____ and the County of _____ for a period of more than six (6) months.

2.  That the parties were married on _____ and they separated on _____, and the petitioner is not pregnant.

3.  That during the course of their marriage there was/were _____ child(ren) born to the parties, namely:

Name and address

_____

_____

4.  That the marriage has suffered irretrievable breakdown.

WHEREFORE, the petition prays that a dissolution of the marriage be granted, and that the petitioner be granted the custody of the minor child(ren); that an order be issued against the respondent, _____, for their support and maintenance; that the respondent be ordered to pay petitioner's attorney a reasonable fee for prosecution of this action; that the Court make an equitable distribution of the property of the parties; and for all other proper relief.

_____

JONES, JONES & JONES

_____

Attorney

STATE OF _____ )
              ) SS:
COUNTY OF _____ )

_____, being first duly sworn upon oath, deposes and says that she is the petitioner in the above-entitled cause and that the facts stated herein above are true as she verily believes.

_____

Petitioner

Subscribed and sworn to before me this _____ day of _____, 19___.

_____
Notary Public

My Commission Expires:

_____

_____
Attorney for Petitioner

Jones, Jones & Jones
Attorneys at Law
2220 _____
Indianapolis, Indiana 46208
Phone # _____

## RESPONSIVE DECLARATION

| Name, Address and Telephone Number of Attorney(s) | Space Below for Use of Court Clerk Only |
|---|---|
| Attorney(s) for ..................... | |

| SUPERIOR COURT OF _____ COUNTY OF _____ | |
|---|---|
| In re the marriage of | CASE NUMBER |
| Petitioner: | RESPONSIVE DECLARATION RE: |
| and | ☒ ORDER TO SHOW CAUSE |
| Respondent: | ☒ NOTICE OF MOTION |

| MANDATORY FORM FOR RESPONSE TO O.S.C. (or MOTION) | Hearing date:   Department/Room No: |
|---|---|

CHILD CUSTODY. I _____ that custody be awarded as requested.
(consent/do not consent)
     Instead, I consent that custody be awarded (specify, including name, birth-date and age of each child):

VISITATION. I _____ that visitation be ordered as requested.
                    (consent/do not consent)
    Instead, I consent that visitation be ordered as follows:

CHILD SUPPORT. I _____ if used for Wife as Respondent change to
                        (consent/do not consent)
read "Accept" [to pay] child support as requested.
    Instead, I consent to pay $_____ monthly for child support, payable
_____.
(weekly/monthly/etc.)

| Name, birthdate and age of each child | Amount |
|---|---|
| (Form can't be used to request | $ _____ |
| Affirmative relief; Must file | _____ |
| own O.S.C. with supporting papers.) | _____ |

SPOUSAL SUPPORT. I _____ [to pay] spousal support as requested. (If
                          (consent/do not consent)
used for wife as respondent, change to read "accept.")
    Instead, I consent to pay $_____ monthly for spousal support, payable
_____.
(weekly/monthly/etc.)

# CHAPTER 11

# Working with a Real Estate Transaction

*In order to be an effective paralegal in the area of real estate procedures and transactions, you must know what is expected of you, and what duties you can perform in this highly specialized area without infringing upon the practice of law. This chapter will help you and your attorney resolve these questions.*

## INTRODUCTION

Your duties in a law office with a heavy real estate practice will be, for the most part, a matter of constant scheduling, keeping up-to-date records and statute of limitation periods as to when documents have to be and should be filed; preparing and checking to determine if all the necessary and required elements have been included in any purchase and sale agreement and/or contract; preparing all required legal documents and instruments of conveyance; and seeing that all necessary instruments have been prepared and processed for the closing of any real estate transaction.

To this end, this chapter sets forth a checklist for the above, and step-by-step procedures to be taken to insure accuracy and completeness of the transaction.

### Reminder

Instruments of conveyance are those documents which:
1) Relate to property, real or personal;
2) Effect title to property, real or personal;
3) Set forth the full description of property, real or personal; and
4) Are entitled to recordation under existing laws.

Typical instruments of conveyance are deeds and mortgages which convey ownership in property and set forth how it is held, such as joint tenancy, tenants in common, community property, and so forth. The deeds you most often work with are the Grant Deed, the Quitclaim Deed, and the Trust Deed.

In conveying property by way of a deed, recall that it should contain the following:

1) Name of grantor;
2) Words of conveyance, i.e., "I give," "I hereby grant, sell or transfer";
3) Name of grantee;
4) Complete description of property being conveyed;
5) Signature of the grantor;
6) Date on which signature was affixed; and
7) A notary acknowledgment of said signature.

*Practical Hint:* When conveying property, the grantor must use the same name as when he or she received the property, such as "D. Bard Smythe to Mary Smythe"—then—"Mary Smythe to James Oslow"—*NOT* "Mary Smith to James Oslow."

As the deed relates to mortgages, recall that the elements of a mortgage are as follows:

1) The mortgagor is the debtor who retains title; and
2) The mortgagee is the lender and acquires a lien on the property.

This document should contain the operative words of the mortgage, a description of the property, and of course, the obligation.

## CHECKLIST FOR RECORDING
## INSTRUMENTS OF CONVEYANCE

1. Make certain that all lines on the document are filled in. Any blanks should be lined through and then initialed by the parties. A notary tape #819 may be used to protect the document from alterations after it has been notarized.

2. Check to see that the party's notarized signature is consistent with the way it appears in the document. It should be legible and written in ink.

3. The proper and appropriate dates should be written in the appropriate spaces in ink.

4. All items on the document, including signatures, the notary seal, and so forth, should be photographically reproducible.

5. Any corrections or alterations should be initialed by the party and the notary to prevent any questions or possible misunderstandings later on. If it is indicated that a loose acknowledgment form (or jurat) is required on the document, make sure that it does not cover up any writing. You might wish to use staples or notary tape #819 to attach the form to the side of a document to avoid the need for removing it during microfilming.

6. Use a seal embosser in addition to a rubber stamp seal to prevent the addition or exchanging of pages to the documents. You should apply the embosser so that all pages receive the indentations in the same location.

> *Hint:* Be sure to double-check to see that all signatures have been affixed to the document and all pertinent dates have been placed on it; as well as the complete legal descriptions set forth on all conveyance documents, including the notarization and notary seal.

## DEVELOPING AN UNLAWFUL DETAINER COMPLAINT

Sooner or later, in working with a real estate problem, disputes will arise necessitating the filing of a lawsuit to resolve the matter, i.e., quiet title actions, partition suits and, one of the most common, the unlawful detainer action. It is on the latter that we focus our attention.

Traditionally, these cases are usually heard in the Municipal Court, and in some jurisdictions may be heard in the Justice Courts. You are cautioned to check your local Court Rules as to this procedure. The monetary jurisdiction can be anywhere from $300 to $5,000; and any sum or damages over these amounts will automatically place the action in the Superior Court of monetary jurisdiction.

As indicated above, Municipal Courts have jurisdiction to try unlawful detainer actions, even in some states where the answer attacks plaintiff's title, provided the attack is directed to the validity of a trustee's sale. However, if the attack is directed to some defect in the Trust Deed, such as forgery or fraud in the inception, creating or opening up the broad question of the title to the property, the Municipal Court would not have jurisdiction. Because of this variance from state to state, check your local Court Rules for the correct procedure in developing an unlawful detainer action based upon the above facts.

## Step-by-Step Procedure

1. Describe the Trust Deed, including recording data, legal description and so forth.

(a) Allege the trustor's default;
(b) Allege recording of Notice of Default in the county where the property is located, including all pertinent data;
(c) Allege notice of default identified in the Trust Deed;
(d) Set forth the book and page where trustee is recorded along with legal description of the property;
(e) Spell out the breach of the obligation;
(f) The nature of the breach; and
(g) Whether or not there is an election to satisfy the obligation.

2. Allege the publication of a Notice to Sell, with copy attached that states the time and place of sale, the fact that the same was advertised and posted, specifying dates of advertising and place of posting.

3. Set forth the names of persons notified by virtue of a specific request subsequent to recordation and prior to the recording of the Notice of Default.

4. Allege that the trustee did in fact mail Notice and that a second mailing of Notice of Sale was sent within the prescribed statutory period.

5. Allege that pursuant to said Notice of Sale plaintiff was the highest bidder, and that upon payment of said sum so bidded, the trustee issued the plaintiff the deed which recited all legal requirements in compliance with the applicable code.

6. Allege that personal service of a Three-Day Notice to Quit was made on defendant, and attach a copy of said Notice and Return of Service.

7. Allege that defendant has failed to surrender possession and remains in possession.

8. Allege the rental value of the premises per month, which does not exceed the Court's jurisdiction.

9. Allege that plaintiff has suffered damages in the sum of $_____, and continues to sustain damages in the sum of $_____ per diem, and

10. End with the normal Prayer for judgment in the favor of plaintiff.

## Preparing Your Attorney's File for Default
## Against Defendant in an Unlawful Detainer Action

1. Secure certified copy of deed;
2. Copy of Three-Day Notice to Quit;
3. Affidavit of service of Three-Day Notice.

## Preparing Your Attorney's File in a Contested Action

Obtain the following:
1. Certified copy of Trust Deed;
2. Copy of Three-Day Notice to Quit;
3. Testimony of service of Three-Day Notice to Quit;
4. Evidence that defendant remains in possession of the premises;
5. Rental value and estimate of damages sustained.

All of the above can be done by way of depositions and/or inter-rogatories; or any other discovery process you and your attorney may determine is applicable.

## 14 FUNCTIONAL DUTIES OF A LEGAL ASSISTANT WORKING WITH A PARTNERSHIP AND PURCHASE/SALE AGREEMENT

## Introduction

Often, in a law office with a heavy real estate practice, clients will come in wanting to enter into a partnership situation in order to buy real property. To this end, you would have to prepare not only a Partnership Agreement, but a Purchase and Sale Agreement for the transfer of real property as well.

Since the Partnership Agreement is boilerplate, and your office may already have its own form, and the setting up of a business entity is discussed elsewhere in this Manual, we have only set hereinbelow for your review, a checklist of duties to be performed by you in following through on a Purchase and Sale Agreement.

1. After your attorney has held the initial meeting with the client, use a checklist of questions and basic information to review and complete

any unanswered questions. If you do not have such a checklist, develop one from your attorney's notes in the file.

2. State your research relating to the tax ramifications of a real estate transaction as well as the legal aspects. (The tax ramifications should have been secured from a Certified Public Accountant and the legal aspects should come from your attorney.)

3. Develop, and then prepare, a time and responsibility schedule to aid you and your attorney to keep on top of such things as when documents should be placed in escrow; when money due from the lender should be on hand; when title should be done or received from the title company, and so forth.

4. Prepare your Partnership Agreement and the Purchase/Sale Agreement per instructions and notes of your attorney.

5. After these have been approved, redraft the agreement, have them typed in final form and mailed out to the parties concerned, for their signatures. During the interim period, begin to gather your exhibits to be attached to the purchase/sale agreement, i.e., plot plans, schedules; assignments of leases; subleases; notes, deeds of trust; minutes, and the like.

> *Note*: Some of these exhibits you may have to prepare, such as your employee agreements and certain other contracts.

6. These exhibits could thereafter be circulated for signature and returned to your office.

7. Prepare your escrow instructions. Note that in some jurisdictions these may be in printed form.

8. After the above has been accomplished, draft your consent to assignment, subleases and estoppel certificate. This latter document may also be a printed form. Be sure to check your local code for this procedure.

9. Send out a Request for a Preliminary Title Report from the applicable title company.

10. Once this package has been executed by all parties have the Certificate of Partnership recorded in the county where the property is located.

> *Note*: As with all voluminous documents, check and recheck to see that every page requiring a signature has been signed; and every page requiring notarization has been so notarized.

11. Then draft any and all remaining documents needed to be deposited into escrow.

12. Draft any and all closing documents needed to close the matter for signature to all the partners, buyer and seller.

13. Coordinate the activities relating to transfer of licenses and permits.

14. Prepare and file with the proper authority the Fictitious Business Name Statement for the partnership.

## OTHER FUNCTIONAL DUTIES YOU CAN PERFORM WHEN WORKING WITH A REAL ESTATE TRANSACTION

1. Prepare leases of all types, including standard residential, commercial and net leases, for residential, office, commercial, industrial property and shopping centers.

2. Draft complaints, answers, demurrers and other documentation for unlawful detainer proceedings as well as documentation relating to attachments and undertakings.

3. Prepare documentation for zoning relief through administrative and court procedures.

4. Prepare various types of secured transaction agreements.

5. Assemble information for obtaining institutional loans.

6. Obtain information and prepare documentation for settlement or closing of purchase or mortgage.

7. Prepare documentation for cooperative housing corporations, condominiums and real estate investment trusts.

8. Prepare closing documents.

### Preparing a Homestead Document

Homestead legislation is designed to protect a family and provide a home for its members wherein they can enjoy the comforts of a home, free from fear of loss either by virtue of their own improprieties or at the will of creditors. To aid you in determining the feasibility and type of homestead which can be recorded on behalf of a client, general character, elements and factors affecting the exercise of a homestead right are as follows:

1. Marital and family qualifications needed for entitlement to the homestead exemption, such as verification of marriage, number of members in family, etc.

2. Wife's right to select homestead, if husband fails to do so.

3. Value and size of land claimable as homestead.

4. Nature of interest in the land or type of property to which homestead exemptions may apply.

5. Nature of date of accrual of debts against which the exemption is inoperative.

6. Mandatory requirements of a formal homestead declaration or application for exemption.

7. Effect of the homestead character of the land upon pre-existing or subsequent attachments or judgment liens.

8. Cut-off date for assertion of the homestead exemption during the enforcement process.

9. Methods to be pursued by the creditors to reach an excess in acreage or value.

10. Loss of exemption because of removal (abandonment) or divorce.

11. Status of proceeds from sale or insurance and/or rents and profits from homestead.

Consider the following form in complying with the above checklist for preparing a homestead.


### DESIGNATION OF HOMESTEAD

THE STATE OF _____
COUNTY OF _____


BEFORE ME, the undersigned authority, a Notary Public in and for said County and State, on this day personally appeared _____ and wife, _____, known to me to be the persons whose names are subscribed hereto, who, after having been by me first duly sworn upon their oaths, deposed and said:

Our names are _____ and _____ and we are husband and wife. We now reside at _____ County, _____, and designate such property as our sole and only homestead property which we own and as to which we and our family are entitled under the Consititution and laws of the State of _____ exempt from forced sale, and we further declare that said property is all of the property and is the only property to which we are now entitled as a homestead exempt from forced sale.

We hereby stipulate and acknowledge by this designation that we have fully utilized and expended all homestead rights in the maximum amount to which we are entitled under the Constitution and laws of the State of _____ exempt from forced sale, and that we have no business homestead and have no rights thereto.

We have simultaneously herewith executed and delivered a Promissory Note in the principal amount of _____ Dollars ($_____) payable to the order of _____, together with a Deed of Trust conveying to _____, Trustee, the following described property, to wit:

The property conveyed by the above mentioned Deed of Trust constitutes no part of our homestead, either residential or business, and we hereby renounce and disclaim any homestead claims in and to said property.

We understand that the funds represented by the above mentioned Note will be disbursed in reliance on the statements herein made and but for the truth of such statement such funds would not be disbursed.

_____

_____

SUBSCRIBED AND SWORN TO before me by _____ and _____ this _____ day of _____.

_____
Notary Public in and for
_____ County, _____

The following Trustee's Deed form is submitted to reinforce the importance of spelling out succinctly the legal description of property so that the same would not fail should prosecution of a real property claim on behalf of your attorney's client become necessary. Oftentimes, these pertinent points are either omitted or transposed; and in some instances, may describe the wrong property.

Hence, you are cautioned to check and recheck such legal descriptions, recorded volume and file numbers. This careful scrutiny also applies to mortgages, deeds of trust and promissory notes, which are based on a piece of real property.

TRUSTEE'S DEED

THE STATE OF _____

KNOW ALL MEN BY

COUNTY OF _____        THESE PRESENTS:

WHEREAS, by a certain Deed of Trust dated _____, 197__, [recorded in Volume _____, Page _____, of the _____. [Filed under File Number _____ and recorded at Film Code Reference Number _____ of the Official Public.] Records of _____ County, _____, _____, as Grantor, conveyed to the undersigned, as Trustee, certain real property hereinafter described, for the purpose of securing and enforcing payment of a certain Note described in said Deed of Trust, of even date therewith and in the original principal sum of $_____; and

WHEREAS, _____, the present owner and holder of said Note and Deed of Trust, requested the undersigned, as Trustee, to enforce the trust, the said Grantors, having made default in the payment of said Note when due and there being due theron the principal sum of _____, plus interest and attorney's fees as provided in said Note; and

WHEREAS, I, as Trustee did on the _____ day of _____, 197__, after having posted written notices of the time, place and terms of a public sale of the hereinafter described property, which written notices were posted at three public places in _____ County, _____, the County in which said real estate is situated, one of which notices was posted at the courthouse door of said County, and which said notices were posted for three consecutive weeks prior to the day of the sale, sell the hereinafter described property at public vendue, at the courthouse door of _____ County, _____, to _____, he being the highest bidder, for the sum of $_____:

NOW, THEREFORE, in consideration of the premises and of the payment to me of the sum of $_____, by the said _____, I, as Trustee, by virtue of the authority conferred upon me in said Deed of Trust, have GRANTED, SOLD AND CONVEYED, and by these presents do GRANT, SELL AND CONVEY, unto the said _____, his heirs and assigns, all of the [following described real property situated in _____ County, _____:] [property located in _____ County, _____, more fully described on Exhibit "A" attached hereto and by this reference incorporated herein.]

TO HAVE AND TO HOLD the above described premises and property, together with the rights, privileges and appurtenances thereto belonging, unto the said _____, his heirs and assigns forever; and I, as said Trustee, do hereby bind the said _____, their heirs, executors and administrators,

to warrant and forever defend the said premises unto the said _____,
his heirs and assigns forever, against the claim or claims, of all persons claiming or
to claim the same or any part thereof.

     EXECUTED this _____ day of _____, 197__.

                      TRUSTEE

                    _____

                    [APPROPRIATE
                    ACKNOWLEDGMENTS WILL
                    BE ADDED]

    A glossary follows on the next page.

## GLOSSARY

### Common Law Mortgage:

     1. Conveyed the land to the mortgagee during the term of the mortgage.

     2. Title to the land was to vest in the mortgagor on payment of the debt secured; if there was a default, the title to the land was absolute as to the mortgagor.

     This would not discharge the debt. The mortgagee could show the deed and recover a judgment and collect the deed in addition to keeping the land.

### Equity of Redemption:

     This is a real property interest; and a right that the buyer has in the property. It is a real property right which must be redeemed within a reasonable time, provided the mortgagee had no control over the cause of the default.

### Foreclosure:

     This is the process by which all further rights existing in the mortgagor are defeated and lost. These proceedings are regulated by statute. Such as:

        1. Strict foreclosure;
        2. Action and sale;
        3. Power of sale.

     As to *strict foreclosure:* A decree of strict foreclosure of a mortgage finds the amount due under the mortgage, orders its payment within a certain limited time, and provides that, in default of such payment, the debtor's right and equity of redemption shall be forever barred and foreclosed. Its effect is to vest title of the property absolutely in the mortgagee, on default in payment, without any sale of the property.

     As to *action and sale:* A lawsuit must be brought; all who have an interest in the property must be made party-defendants; case must be tried; judgment must be entered and the property sold. Proceeds of the sale are applied to the debt and the surplus given to the mortgagor (a default judgment is entered against the mortgagor.)

As to *power of sale:* Must be expressly conferred on the mortgagee by the terms of the mortgage. No court action is required. But a notice of sale must be given to the mortgagor and the sale advertised. The sale must be at an auction and conducted fairly and an effort made to sell the property at the highest price obtainable with the right of redemption.

## General Contractor:

The general contractor is the person who has contracted for the job. A subcontractor is the person who has contracted with the general contractor to do a stipulated portion of a job. The material man is the person who has contracted the material for the job.

## Guarantor:

This person does not join in making a promise. His liability arises on the happening of an event: a stipulated event, such as the failure of the principal to perform; or the insolvency of the principal. It is collateral to the promise and *unenforceable unless, it is in writing*. This, too, is created by contract.

## Land Contract:

Seller agrees to sell, and the buyer agrees to buy and pay a stipulated and/or agreed purchase price which is set out in a contract. Note that the purchaser is the equitable owner; the seller holds the legal title and does not deed the property to the purchaser until the full purchase price has been paid. In case of default, if there is a voluntary surrender of the property, the seller takes absolute title and possession of the property and the buyer's equity will be cut off.

## Mortgage:

Conveys an interest in real property and is executed with the same formality as a deed. Otherwise, it cannot be recorded. An unrecorded mortgage is invalid against a bona fide purchaser or a mortgagee's full value if they have no notice or knowledge of the mortgage; or against creditors who acquire a lien on the property.

## Mortgagor (Owner):

May sell the property without the consent of the mortgagee
(loaner); has the right to any surplus land or property if sold at a foreclosure
proceeding; cannot assign his or her liability.

## Right of Contribution:

When there are two or more sureties for the same principal and for
the same obligation, and one pays the entire obligation or more than his
share, he becomes entitled to reimbursement from co-sureties for the
amount paid over and above his share.

## Right of Subrogation, Surety's:

In the acquiring, the operation in law, all the rights of the creditor
are against the principal, if he, the surety, is compelled to perform the
obligation of the principal. This right does not arise until the creditor has
been paid in full.

## Surety:

A person who is liable for the payment of another's debt; or for the
performance of another's duty. If required to perform, he is entitled to
reimbursement from his principal for any loss. Surety and principal together become the obligee to pay or perform. This is normally created by
contract.

# Bankruptcy

*This chapter not only gives you an explanation of the various types of petitions which can be filed by individuals and business entities, but sets forth the step-by-step procedures for preparing and filing these petitions as well.*

CHAPTER 12

## INTRODUCTION

Remember that the need to file a bankruptcy proceeding is a great emotional burden as well as a financial embarrassment to your attorney's client. It therefore goes without saying that your role as legal assistant is one of great importance, requiring a great deal of compassion, understanding, and of course, meticulous and skillful handling.

As you know, bankruptcy proceedings are held in the United States District Courts,[1] in a designated district in your state. You should therefore look to the Federal Rules of Civil Procedure for guidelines, paying particular attention to the rules relating to the Bankruptcy Act as found in Title 28, United States Code, Chapter 131, Section 2075.

The name of the game in bankruptcy is schedules, schedules, schedules; checking and rechecking for accuracy in balances due and owing; and correct grand totals of debts owed by the client.

## TEN TRIED AND PROVEN PRACTICAL
## STEP-BY-STEP PROCEDURES:

1) After the initial interview between your attorney and the client, your conference with the client should be held.

---

[1] Note that under the Bankruptcy Code, separate Bankruptcy Courts have been established for the various Districts throughout the United States. (See 11 U.S.C. §11.)

2) In gathering the data needed as set forth in the functional duties hereinabove, be sure to obtain the following:

   a) Name
   b) Address
   c) Telephone number
   d) Social Security number
   e) Marital status (if a woman, her maiden name, together with date of marriage(s); if divorced, the date of legal separation, and/or entry of Final Divorce Decree.

3) Obtain a complete list of any and all debts outstanding, current or in arrears, long past due or delinquent.

4) Thereafter, discreetly check to see if the facts given to you are in fact correct by calling the creditors.

5) Check the judgment section of the court to determine if there are any outstanding judgments or lawsuits pending against the client.

6) If you determine that one of the creditors is a member of the family, verify the debt owed, obtain documentation if required, and discuss the matter with your attorney to protect the client from a "preference suit" at a later date.

7) If real property is involved, be sure to obtain the legal description and that the same is correct. (This data will enable you to complete the filing of a Declaration of Homestead on behalf of the client if that has not been done.)

8) After the above and foregoing has been accomplished, recheck the debts with the client before filing.

9) A suggested office procedure for verifying information with the client is to make a copy of the completed petition and mail the same to the client for study. We have found that a week's follow-up is recommended in these situations.

10) Finally, check and recheck; and check again, to determine if the client has signed each and every page required, and that those pages requiring notarization have been notarized. It is now time to file the same with the Bankruptcy Court with the appropriate filing fee.

## REMINDERS

1.  Chapter VIII applies to railroad reorganization. In this instance you should prepare and file the original and two copies of the Petition, with any exhibits and the like being attached and filed in duplicate.

2.  Chapter X applies to bankruptcy proceedings for a corporate reorganization and the original Petition with four copies should be filed, with any additional documents or exhibits being filed in quadruplicate.

3.  Chapter XI applies to bankruptcy proceedings for arrangements as to corporations and railroads. Here you should file the original Petition and two copies with all other documentation being filed in duplicate.

4.  Chapter XII is applicable where the arrangement or bankruptcy proceeding involves real property. You should file the original Petition plus two copies, with duplicate copies of any and all exhibits being filed.

5.  Chapter XIII, Wage Earner Petitions, should be filed in triplicate with any and all papers, if applicable, in duplicate.

*Note*: In some jurisdictions the wage earner may be asked if he intends to reaffirm the debt after he has been adjudged a bankrupt. You should check with your attorney regarding this procedure and whether or not it is the intention of the client to do so.

## BASIC FUNCTIONAL DUTIES OF A PARAPROFESSIONAL WORKING WITH A BANKRUPTCY PETITION

1.  Collect personal financial information about the bankrupt.

2.  Compile initial bankruptcy schedules.

3.  Survey court records of lawsuits and judgments against the bankrupt, if any.

4.  File bankruptcy schedules and appropriate fee with bankruptcy court.

5.  Collect and organize data for bankruptcy hearing, (other than wage earner).

6. Collect data for creditors' proofs of claim regarding bankrupt, (other than wage earner).

7. Complete credit proof of claim regarding bankruptcy, (other than wage earner).

8. Compile initial schedules for bankrupt wage earner plan.

9. File wage earner plan schedule with bankruptcy court.

10. Collect information for bankruptcy hearing.

11. Compile data for credit proof for wage earner plan.

12. Write a proof of claim for wage earner plan.

*Note*: Check and recheck; and check again, to determine if the client has signed each and every page required; and that those pages requiring notarization have been notarized. This, because too many times petitions are returned by the court merely for lack of a signature. This can be crucial if time is of the essence.

The following forms are provided for illustrative purposes.


### APPLICATION TO STAY STATE COURT ACTION


Attorney Information

#### COURT INFORMATION

In the Matter of                                  No.

                                    )
                                    )        APPLICATION TO STAY STATE
                                    )        COURT ACTION
                                    )
        Bankrupt                    )
_____)


The application of _____, bankrupt herein, respectfully represents and shows as follows:

1. Applicant is the above named bankrupt, and filed a voluntary petition in bankruptcy on the _____ day of _____.

2. That on the date of the filing of said voluntary petition of bankruptcy, there were pending against the applicant the following actions as indicated hereinbelow:

NAME OF PLAINTIFF:                      COURT            CASE NO.
(Here the legal assistant should list any and all pending litigated matters against the bankrupt, including the name of the plaintiff, the court and the case number.)

3. Each of the above actions is based upon a claim of a type provable in bankruptcy and as to which a discharge in bankruptcy would be barred. Unless said actions are stayed as to your applicant until the question of his right to a discharge is determined, your applicant will be deprived of benefits to which he is entitled under the provisions of the Bankruptcy Act.

WHEREFORE, your applicant prays that this court enter its order staying the above referred to actions pending determination of your applicant's right to a discharge in bankruptcy.

_____
Attorney Signature

## ANSWER OF RESPONDENT TO APPLICATION
## TO STAY STATE COURT ACTION

Attorney Information

### COURT INFORMATION

| In the matter of | ) | No. |
| | ) | |
| | ) | ANSWER OF RESPONDENT _____ |
| | ) | TO APPLICATION TO STAY STATE |
| | ) | COURT ACTION |
| | ) | |
| Bankrupt. | ) | |

COMES NOW _____, and files his answer as follows:

1. With respect to that certain action now pending in the superior court in and for the county of _____, State of _____, entitled _____ v _____, and being case No. ____, this answering respondent denies that said action is based upon a claim of a type dischargeable in bankruptcy, and denies that the bankrupt is entitled to a stay of said proceedings.

WHEREFORE, this answering respondent prays that the temporary restraining order heretofore issued as to him be dissolved, and that an order be entered denying the bankrupt's application to stay state court action as to this answering respondent.

_____
Attorney Signature

In line with the aforementioned discussion of filing bankruptcy petitions on behalf of your client, consider the following forms as a guide in preparing such petition.

The first form deals with a Creditor's Petition for Bankruptcy for your comparison to an individual wage earner or corporate entity Petition in Bankruptcy.

If you are the attorney for the creditor, the above, and following forms will be of value to you. Note that the objections to the discharge form and contents require specific information which will utilize your ''gathering of information'' abilities to aid you in preparing the financial documentation required.

*Note*: The Petition in Bankruptcy for wage earners is normally a printed form, hence, the same is not included herein.

## CREDITORS' PETITION FOR BANKRUPTCY

### CAPTION

1. Petitioners, _____, all _____, and _____ of _____, are creditors of _____ of the City of _____, having provable claims against said bankrupt, not contingent as to liability, amounting in the aggregate, in excess of the value of the securities held by them, to $500.00 or over. The nature and amount of petitioners' claims are as follows:

_____

_____

2. The alleged bankrupt has had his principal place of business (or has resided) within this district for the past (6) months preceding the filing of this petition.

3. The alleged bankrupt owes debts in the amount of $1.000 or more and is a person who may be adjudged an involuntary bankrupt under the Bankruptcy Act.

4. Within the past four months preceding the filing of this petition, the alleged bankrupt committed an act of bankruptcy in that he did on _____.

WHEREFORE, petitioners pray that _____ be adjudged as a bankrupt under the Act.

_____

Attorney for Petitioners

_____
_____

Address

_____
_____

Petitioners

STATE OF _____ )
                           ) SS
COUNTY OF _____ )

    I, _____, one of the petitioners in the foregoing petition, do hereby swear that the statements contained therein are true according to the best of my knowledge, information and belief.

_____

Petitioner

Subscribed and sworn to before me on _____, 19__.

_____

Notary

## SPECIFICATION OF OBJECTIONS TO DISCHARGE

Attorney Information

### UNITED STATES DISTRICT COURT

FOR THE _____ DISTRICT OF _____

_____ DIVISION

In the Matter of      )   No.
                  )
                  )   SPECIFICATION OF OBJECTIONS
                  )   TO DISCHARGE
                  )
        Bankrupt. )
                  )
_____ )

COMES NOW _____ a creditor of the above named bankrupt and objects to the bankrupt's discharge under Section _____ of the Bankruptcy Act as follows:

1. While engaged in the business as a sole proprietor under the name of _____, said bankrupt on or about the _____ day of _____, obtained such business property on credit by making or publishing a materially false statement and writing respecting his financial condition.

2. Attached hereto and incorporated herein by reference is a copy of said financial statement dated the _____ day of _____.

3. Said financial statement was materially raised, in that the bankrupt overstated the value of his equipment by the sum of _____ ($____) Dollars, and in that the said bankrupt failed to reflect, as a liability, a debt in the amount of approximately _____ ($____) Dollars then owing to the bankrupt's father, Mr. _____.

WHEREFORE, the objector prays that this court enter its order denying the discharge of bankruptcy of the above named bankrupt.

_____

# CHAPTER 13

# Working with Industrial Claims

*This chapter is designed to give you an overview of the "black letter" law governing industrial claims and the steps used in prosecuting them; as well as the various claims which can be filed on behalf of your attorney's client.*

191

## INTRODUCTION

If there is any area of the law where a legal assistant can be of extreme value to the practicing attorney, it is the area of Workmen's Compensation law and procedures.

Nowhere in the area of law is there a more personalized suffering sustained by an entire family. The misery and pain inflicted upon the family of the injured employee, when he or she becomes unemployable because of an industrial accident, cannot be measured in damages for "pain and suffering" as in the accepted personal injury cases. In many cases, these individuals are maimed for life, or at the very least, aren't able to secure gainful employment in the same or similar job activity. In most cases, the adverse residual effects of an industrial injury will remain throughout a lifetime.

In order to properly interview a client and complete applicable claim forms, and follow the industrial claim to a successful conclusion, you, as the legal assistant, must know and have a thorough understanding of Workmen's Compensation law and how it operates. To this end, recall the following:

A. An industrial accident is normally any accident occurring on the job while in the course and scope of employment.

193

FOR EXAMPLE:

If you are employed in a grocery store and it is your job to put away heavy bags of potatoes; or lift heavy slabs of meat; or boxes of canned goods from one place to another within the store, and in doing any of the above, you injure your back or sustain a severe strain or sprain of a muscle while performing said duties, all of which necessitate medical treatment or hospitalization, this is an "on-the-job injury" entitling you to file an industrial accident claim before the Industrial Accident Board.

B. An industrial illness, on the other hand, may include any injury or disease which is caused or aggravated by a person's work or working conditions and may include damage to artificial limbs, dentures, hearing aids, eyeglasses, and the like. It is incidental to the injury.

Examples of industrial illnesses are:

    a. Chemical poisoning;
    b. Lung poisoning;
    c. Stress or strain which may aggravate arthritis;
    d. Latent diabetes;
    e. Psychological problems, and the like.

The above and foregoing illnesses are classified as follows:

    a. *Specific:* Occurring as the result of one incident or exposure;
    b. *Cumulative:* Occurring repeatedly over an extended period of traumatic activities, which combination causes a disability;
    c. *Occupational disease:* One in which the cumulative effects of continuous exposure to the harmful elements of one's employment result in disability, as in the stress and strain of your back and the chemical poisoning mentioned above.

C. An industrial accident claim is filed against the Worker's Compensation insurance carrier of the employer. IT IS NOT A CLAIM AGAINST THE EMPLOYER PER SE, BUT AGAINST HIS WORKER'S COMPENSATION INSURANCE CARRIER.

## I. INFORMAL PROCEDURES:

## A. Notice of Claim

The particulars to look for, pinpoint and calendar, are as follows:

1. The date of the injury (or the last day of treatment) to avoid expiration of the statute of limitations.

2. Determine whether the applicant is receiving medical treatment; if so,

3. Has your office received up-to-date medical reports?

4. Is the applicant receiving temporary disability payments in a timely manner based upon his weekly salary?

5. Have temporary disability payments been terminated; if so, why?

6. Is the insurance company providing the necessary medication?

7. Is the applicant being reimbursed for out-of-pocket expenses for round trip mileage to and from the insurance company doctor?

8. Have all of these dates for follow-up been placed on your calendar and your boss's calendar, and on the file, if applicable?

## B. Processing the Compromise and Release

If, after the Notice of Claim has been filed, and the parties agree to settle the matter out of court by means of a Compromise and Release, then be concerned with the following:

1. The insertion of the attorney's fees;

2. The reason and purpose for the Compromise and Release;

3. Obtain a waiver from the applicable Department of Unemployment (or such other applicable agency in your state) as to its lien, if applicable;

4. Check the liens against the gross settlement figure to make sure they are accurate; and

5. Obtain the approval and signature of the applicant.

6. Then follow the normal procedure for having Compromise and Release filed with the court and other parties involved.

## II. CHECKLIST FOR FORMAL PROCEDURES:

| Document | Statute of Limitations |
| --- | --- |
| Initial Application | 1 year from date of injury or last date of treatment. |
| Answer | Based on common practice and procedure. |
| Continuous Trauma | May be filed at the time |

| Document | Statute of Limitations |
|---|---|
| (Cumulative Industrial) | of initial application and based on a 1-year disability and knowledge thereof that it is work-related. |
| Death Benefits | 1 year from date of death. |
| Industrial Diseases | 1 year from date of discovery. |
| Minor's Incompetent Claim | Time does not begin to run against a minor or incompetent until a Guardian Ad Litem or Trustee has been appointed. |
| New and Further Disability (and Permanent Disability) | 5 years from date of injury. |
| Petition for Computation of funds | Can be filed at any time after receipt of Findings and Award. |
| Petition for Reconsideration | May be filed within 20 days after receipt of Findings and Award. |
| Petition to Reopen | Within 5 years of the date of injury. |
| Serious and Willful Application | 1 year from date of injury. |
| Subsequent Injuries Fund | May be filed at the time of the initial application; and though in dispute, within 5 years of industrial injury. (This procedure may be peculiar only to the State of California: check your local state statutes on this.) |
| Writ of Review (Appeal) | 30 days after denial of Petition for Reconsideration. |

*Note*: You may wish to check your local state statutes on the above procedures since they may or may not be applicable to your state. Caution is also necessary when filing any of the above applications or petitions, and to this end, you should be governed by the policy of the local Worker's Compensation agency and/or state rules and regulations.

In any event, you should prepare the appropriate number of copies and file them with the Worker's Compensation Appeals Board, leave a copy for your file, and as a courtesy, mail a copy to the insurance carrier of the employer.

## STATUTE OF LIMITATIONS CHECKLIST WHEN WORKING WITH A FINDINGS AND AWARD

1. Calendar 20 days to receive monies from the insurance company after issuance of the Findings and Award;

2. Calendar 20 days within which to file a Petition for Reconsideration if the Findings and Award is unsatisfactory;

3. File a Petition of Comutation on behalf of the applicant any time after receipt of the Findings and Award;

4. Calendar a Petition to Reopen the claim noting that the same may be filed within 5 years of the date of the injury. This because the Findings and Award, as you recall, closes the files at this point.

### A Proven Procedure

A yearly 3x5 card index of cases which proceeded to a Findings and Award is the best way to keep abreast of those cases likely to be reopened within a 5-year period. These files should be placed in an "active closed" section of your file cabinet and audited every 6 months, depending on the date of the original injury.

### The Petition to Reopen

This Petition must be filed within 5 years from the date of the injury, and if filed on the last day permissible, the adverse party has the right to seek relief by filing a counter-petition within 30 days of the filing of your Petition to Reopen. This Petition is based on recurring or increased disability (new and further disability); or that the disability has diminished or terminated. (The need for a hearing on this Petition will be determined by the rules of your local Appeals Board or state statutes.)

## Preparing a Petition for Reconsideration

This Petition is an appeal vehicle which must be filed 20 days from the date of the Referee's Decision on the original hearing on the claim. You should check your local rules to verify the time limitation relating to the service of this document on the interested parties to the action.

## Reminders

The grounds upon which you can file a Petition for Reconsideration are as follows:

1. That the Decision was obtained by fraud;
2. That the evidence did not justify the Findings of Fact;
3. That the Findings of Fact did not support the order;
4. That new evidence has been discovered which was undiscoverable at the time of the original hearing; and
5. That the order so rendered exceeded the power of the Appeals Board.

*Cautionary Measure Note:* A Petition for Reconsideration will be denied if you only set forth statutory grounds. Therefore, be sure to make specific reference to the record and supply supporting law and case authority for each allegation.

## Filing Procedure

Prepare and file the original of the Petition with the Appeals Board; serve a copy on the insurance company, or its legal representative, and retain a copy thereof for your file. (Once again, check your local rules of the Appeals Board or state statutes to determine if there is a need for a hearing on this Petition.)

## REVIEW OF FEDERAL LAW AFFECTING WORKERS' COMPENSATION

The practice and procedure for filing or making application under the following federal laws affecting Workers' Compensation benefits may be found in the Federal Code or appropriate administrative agency rules and regulations.

a. Federal Employers' Liability Act refers to Railroad employees. Under the provision of this Act, in a lawsuit brought for injury or death of an employee of a common carrier, the railroad is held to be liable for damages sustained.

b. The Jones Act merely extends the provisions of the Federal Employers' Liability Act to include seamen with the same right to file an action for injury or wrongful death based upon negligence, in whole or in part, on the part of the employer.

c. Federal Compensation Acts:

    (i) The Longshoremen's and Harbor Workers' Compensation Act which provides for medical and hospital services, together with compensation for injury and death, occurring upon the waters of the United States, including any dry dock and maritime employees.

    (ii) The Defense Base Act which applies to persons employed by the military, air or naval base outside the continental United States; and individuals employed in public works in any territory or possession outside of the United States, provided such individuals injured were employed under the contract of a contractor with the United States.

    (iii) The Federal Employers' Compensation Act which provides for compensation benefits to any individual employed by the United States for an injury or death while in the performance of his duties.

While the initial claim in an industrial accident proceeding may be, and often is, a printed form, the time comes when you, as the legal assistant, must draft certain documents from scratch. To this end, consider the following forms as a guide, paying particular notice to the fact that you must include the applicable code sections as a part of your pleading in order to establish the jurisdiction of the Workmen's Compensation Appeals Board. The attached form Application for Award for a Serious and Willful Misconduct of Employer is a typical format in spelling out the sections which are applicable and which have been violated by an employer.

As to the Petition to Reopen for New and Further Disability Based on Change in Condition, it is important that the client be examined and his physical condition and/or injury be re-evaluated by the doctor prior to the filing of the petition, and a copy of such new medical report should be attached thereto before mailing it to opposing counsel and/or insurance company, and to the Workmen's Compensation Insurance Board.

BEFORE THE WORKMEN'S COMPENSATION APPEALS BOARD

STATE OF _____

|  |  |
|---|---|
| ) | NO. |
| ) | |
| _____, ) | PETITION TO REOPEN FOR |
| Applicant, ) | NEW AND FURTHER DIS- |
| vs. ) | ABILITY BASED ON CHANGE |
| ) | IN CONDITION |
| ) | |
| ) | |
| _____, ) | |
| ) | |
| Defendants. ) | |
| ) | |
| _____) | |

COMES NOW your petitioner _____, and respectfully alleges as follows:

I.

Your petitioner sustained an industrial injury to his back, hip and legs on April 27, 19__. As a result of proceedings before the Workmen's Compensation Appeals Board, a Findings and Award was issued in the above matter, awarding your petitioner temporary disability, and permanent disability benefits and medical-legal expenses.

II

Since the date of last evidence in the above entitled case, there has been a change in the petitioner's condition, causing a further period of disability, a need for specific type of medical care and an increase in his permanent disability.

III

In support of the above allegation, we have attached the medical report of Dr. _____, dated August 14, 19__ and by this reference, said medical report is made a part of this petition as though set forth in full herein.

WHEREFORE, your petitioner respectfully prays that this case be set for further proceedings and that thereafter he be awarded further temporary disability benefits, further necessary medical treatment, an increase in permanent disability and the reasonable value of the medical expense necessarily incurred on account of said recurrence of disability.

Dated: September 2, 19__.

_____
Attorneys For Petitioner

APPLICATION FOR AWARD FOR SERIOUS AND
WILLFUL MISCONDUCT OF EMPLOYER

Attorney Information

STATE OF _____
AGRICULTURE AND SERVICES AGENCY
DEPARTMENT OF INDUSTRIAL RELATIONS
DIVISION OF INDUSTRIAL ACCIDENTS
WORKMEN'S COMPENSATION APPEALS BOARD

|  |  |
|---|---|
| ) | CASE NO. |
| ) |  |
| ) | APPLICATION FOR AWARD FOR |
| Applicant, ) | SERIOUS AND WILLFUL |
| ) | MISCONDUCT OF EMPLOYER |
| vs.  ) |  |
| ) |  |
| ) |  |
| ) |  |
| _____ ) |  |
| a corporation, _____ ) |  |
| INSURANCE COMPANY, ) |  |
| ) |  |
| Defendants. ) |  |
| ) |  |
| _____) |  |

Pursuant to Section 10445 of the Workmen's Compensation Appeals Board's Rule of Practice and Procedure, applicant alleges serious and willful misconduct of the employer based on the following theories:

FIRST THEORY
(Failure to Provide Safe Place to Work)

I

Each of the defendants _____ and _____ Insurance Company (hereafter both and each referred to as defendant), was and is at all times herein mentioned a corporation duly organized and existing by and under the laws of the State of _____ with its principal place of business at

_____, _____.

II

On May 21, 19 __, applicant was employed by defendant as a construction worker and was engaged in the performance of his duties within the scope of his employment on the property of _____, _____ County, _____, _____, under the immediate supervision and direction of one _____ and one _____.

### III

On said date, at about 1:25 P.M., applicant was directed by
_____ who was acting as general foreman to operate a skiploader.

### IV

With knowledge of the requirements of Labor Code Sections 6400-6404,
defendant intentionally and willfully and with knowledge that serious injury to
applicant was a probable result, failed to furnish and use safety devices and
safeguards for the benefit of applicant, failed to adopt and use methods and
processes reasonably adequate to render applicant's employment and place of
employment safe, and failed to do those things reasonably necessary to protect the
life and safety of applicant in that:

A. Defendant furnished to applicant and directed applicant to operate a
skiploader which had defective brakes, had a defective rear drag buckset, had a
defective power transmission system, and each of these things, each and all of
which rendered said skiploader likely to go out of control and to crash;

B. With knowledge of the foregoing tendencies of said skiploader, defendant failed to provide proper or any warning to applicant of said tendencies.

### V

As a proximate result of said serious and willful misconduct of defendant,
applicant was stricken with great force and violence when the said skiploader went
out of control and crashed into nearby vehicles and other objects and sustained
injuries resulting in both temporary and permanent disability, causing applicant to
be out of work from May 21, 19__ to the present and continuing indefinitely into
the future, and to receive medical treatment at various times between May 21,
19__ and the present and continuing indefinitely into the future.

### SECOND THEORY
#### (Violation of Industrial Safety Order)

### I

Paragraphs II, III, IIII and IV of the first theory are incorporated herein by
reference.

### II

Title 8, _____ Administrative Code, General Industry Safety
Order, Sections 3653, 3659(a)(z), 3661(a) were each applicable to work being
performed by applicant on May 21, 19__ in that said skiploader and its associated
parts were each within the meaning of one or more terms of said safety order.

### III

The existence and terms of said safety order and the conditions making
it applicable to applicant's work at the time of the injury were known by _____,
_____ and each of them.

IV

Said safety orders were each violated in that:

A. Defendant furnished to applicant and directed applicant to operate a skiploader which had defective brakes, had a defective rear drag buckset, had a defective power transmission system, and each of these things, each and all of which rendered said skiploader likely to go out of control and to crash;

B. With knowledge of the foregoing tendencies of said skiploader, defendant failed to provide proper or any warning to applicant of said tendencies.

V

The violation of said safety orders proximately caused applicant's injury in that applicant was stricken with great force and violence when said skiploader went out of control and crashed into nearby vehicles and other objects while applicant was aboard said machine and sustained injuries resulting in both temporary and permanent disability, causing applicant to be out of work from May 21, 19__ to the present and continuing indefinitely into the future, and to receive medical treatment at various times between May 21, 19__ and the present and continuing indefinitely into the future.

WHEREFORE, applicant requests that he be awarded additional benefits consisting of an increase of one-half in compensation otherwise recoverable, together with costs and expenses.

Executed on _____, 19__, at _____,

_____.


_____

_____

ATTORNEY FOR APPLICANT

# CHAPTER 14

# Working with a Contract Transaction

*As a paralegal, you cannot draft a viable contract unless you know what constitutes a valid contract, and what laws affect them. This chapter addresses itself to these issues and answers them.*

## INTRODUCTION

A breach of contract means that one of the parties has failed and refused to perform under the contract, and without a valid or legal reason. As a result, a cause of action may be based upon this failure to perform.

As a general proposition, parties seeking performance of an agreed-upon contract may either elect to rescind the contract or may simply want to sue to recover money damages; or the value of any services rendered by him under the contract. It should be noted that the injured party has the option to maintain the contract and sue for damages for the breach.

*Tip:* Drafting a contract involves knowing the right thing to worry about!

## PLEADING A BREACH OF CONTRACT

In preparing a pleading involving a breach of contract, you must be direct and to the point using as many theories as you can. The reason for this is if you fail in one, your attorney may be able to win in another. This procedure is used to ensure that the client will come out ''whole.''

FOR EXAMPLE:

Let us say we have an action for specific performance, which forces a seller to sell to a buyer, when the seller decides that he does not want to sell. In this instance, you should draft a complaint to include requests, not only for specific performance of the contract, but also for the return of a deposit, if applicable; and damages for inconvenience as it relates to the buyer, for uprooting his family to move to a location, or putting his furniture in storage until the escrow is completed, and so forth.

Further, you should exercise your option to election of remedies. But in this instance, you should check with your attorney.

FOR EXAMPLE:

Say you are suing on the ground that no valid contract did, in fact, exist. Or, if your suit is being filed seeking rescission of the contract, you may be attempting to disaffirm the contract. In this connection, you should determine the true desire of the client and be sure what it is your attorney wants relative to election of remedies as above-referred to.

Another critical area in pleading a breach of contract is the allegation of, and/or prayer for damages. This cause of action or paragraph, as the case may be, normally occurs and is centered around the ''splitting of actions'' in your Complaint.

FOR EXAMPLE:

Say you prepared for the signature of your attorney, a Complaint in which you are seeking specific performance of a contract and he signed the same without checking it, and it was filed without an allegation or prayer for punitive or exemplary damages. This oversight is termed ''res judicata'' as to your damages, and your attorney cannot go into Court seeking punitive damages or exemplary damages since there was no foundation laid. The doctrine of ''res judicata'' is giving a defense to the cause of action or the ''splitting of actions.''

## PLEADING THE COMMON COUNTS

In most breach of contract cases you are pleading what is commonly called the common counts. These counts are called law relief actions involving contracts for goods sold and delivered, work, labor and services performed; money had and received; and, for accounts stated.

In these Complaints there must be an allegation of breach to show violation of the rights of the plaintiff by the defendant and a statement to the effect that demand for performance, payment and so forth was made; and that defendant failed and refused, and continues to fail and refuse to make the plaintiff "whole."

In these counts, you must allege an express promise to pay or an amount agreed upon as between the parties, together with the reasonable amount of the services, and damages sustained as a result of the breach.

*Caution:* You are cautioned to spell out the demand in the Complaint succinctly and with clarity, since if it leaves the defendant in doubt, or if it is ambiguous, not only will it be subjected to a demurrer, if applicable in your state, but the defendant may make a demand for a Bill of Particulars. This Bill of Particulars would require the plaintiff to set forth a more detailed statement of facts and precisely how the contract was breached, together with a breakdown of the money damages sustained, if applicable.

(Note that this aforementioned procedures relates to California practice, and hence, you should check your local Court Rules to determine if applicable in your jurisdiction. For example, in Alabama, there is no provision for a "Bill of Particulars" but they do have a "Motion for More Definite Statement," which would amount to approximately the same thing as a Bill of Particulars in California.)

## THE COMMON COUNTS

The following common count forms are divided into two sections. The first five examples you will note are as drafted under the Federal Rules of Civil Procedure and the second three common count forms are as drafted under the California Code of Civil Procedure. You should check your own State Code to see whether or not this format is applicable in your state.

### Common Counts

(As Prepared Under the Federal Rules of Civil Proc.)

*Gentle Reminder:* Remember that the allegation of jurisdiction must be included in any complaint filed in the Federal Court Systems.

## EXAMPLES OF JURISDICTION:

A. Jurisdiction founded on diversity of citizenship and amount.

"Plaintiff is a citizen of the State of _____ and Defendant is a corporation incorporated under the laws of the State of _____, having its principal place of business in a state other than the State of _____.
"The matter in controversy exceeds, exclusive of interest and costs, the sum of $15,000.00.''

B. Jurisdiction founded on the existence of a federal question and an amount in controversy.

"The action arises under (the Constitution of the United States, Article _____, Section _____,); or (the _____ Amendment to the Constitution of the United States, Section _____); or (U.S.C., Title _____, Section _____) and so forth, as hereinafter more fully appears.
"The matter in controversy exceeds, exclusive of interest and costs, the sum of $15,000.00''

Hence, the following complaints with common counts would be as follows:

### COMPLAINT FOR GOODS SOLD AND DELIVERED

1. Allegation of jurisdiction.
2. Defendant owes plaintiff _____ dollars for goods sold and delivered by plaintiff and defendant between June 1, _____ and December 1, _____.

WHEREFORE .....

### COMPLAINT FOR MONEY LENT

1. Allegation of jurisdiction.
2. Defendant owes plaintiff _____ dollars for money lent by plaintiff to defendant on April _____, 19__.

WHEREFORE ......

## COMPLAINT FOR MONEY HAD AND RECEIVED

1. Allegation of jurisdiction.
2. Defendant owes plaintiff _____ dollars for money had and received from D.E.L. on April _____, 19__ to be paid by defendant to plaintiff.
WHEREFORE ......

## COMPLAINT FOR MONEY PAID BY MISTAKE

1. Allegation of jurisdiction.
2. Defendant owes plaintiff _____ dollars for money paid by plaintiff to defendant by mistake on April 1, 19__ under the following circumstances: (here state the circumstances according to Federal Rules of Civil Procedure No. 9(b).
WHEREFORE ....

## COMPLAINT ON AN ACCOUNT

1. Allegation of jurisdiction.
2. Defendant owes plaintiff _____ dollars according to the count hereto annexed as Exhibit "A."
WHEREFORE, ...

## ACCOUNTS STATED

Attorney Information

## COURT INFORMATION

Plaintiff, )  NO. _____
             )
vs.          )  ACCOUNTS STATED
             )
Defendant. )
             )
_____ )

Within four years last past, on or about _____, 19__ at _____, an account was stated by and between plaintiff and defendant, wherein and whereby it was agreed that defendant was indebted to plaintiff in the sum of _____.

No part of said sum has been paid.

(And the usual closings as with any other complaint unless you are just filing a common count complaint).

## OPEN BOOK ACCOUNT

Attorney Information

### COURT INFORMATION

| | |
|---|---|
| Plaintiff, ) | No. _____ |
| ) | |
| vs. ) | OPEN BOOK ACCOUNT |
| ) | |
| Defendant. ) | |
| ) | |
| _____) | |

Within four years last past, and on or about _____, 19__ at _____, plaintiff furnished to defendant at his special instance and request, upon an open book account, goods, wares, and merchandise of the aggregate agreed reasonable value of _____.

No part of said sum has been paid (except _____ dollars and there is now due, owing and unpaid _____ dollars).

### WORK AND LABOR
(The reasonable value thereof)

Attorney Information

### COURT INFORMATION

| | |
|---|---|
| ) | Case No. _____ |
| ) | |
| ) | WORK AND LABOR |
| ) | (COMMON COUNT) |
| Parties ) | |
| ) | |
| ) | |
| ) | |
| _____) | |

Suggested paragraphs for the above complaint:

Between and during the period _____, 19__ and _____, 19__ at (here you put the city and state) plaintiff rendered the services to defendant as a (name the type of services rendered, maid, housekeeper, companion, etc.). Such services were so rendered and performed at the instance and request of defendant, and the defendant promised to pay plaintiff the reasonable value of such services.

Plaintiff contends that the reasonable value of said services as a (here designate the type of services rendered) at the time they were rendered and at the time defendant promised to pay, was the sum of $_____.

Defendant alleges that no part of said sum has been paid (here if there has been a sum paid on the account, then set forth the amount that has been paid) (then thereafter set forth the amount that is due and owing minus the sum that has been paid).

## BILL OF PARTICULARS

This document is usually requested by the defendant in a litigated matter and its purpose is to define with specificity the injury and damage alleged by the plaintiff. This request also has a statutory limitation response. You are cautioned to check your local codes for this procedure.

To create this document, you must look to your attorney's notes and the complaint to determine what acts of omission or commission are the basis of the allegations as set forth in the complaint as the wrong, injury or subsequent damage in general terms. For example, what is the actual act of breach of contract; or act of negligence on the part of the defendant which caused the injury, and so forth? A sample Bill of Particulars is given on the next page.

## BILL OF PARTICULARS

Attorneys for Defendant and Cross-Complainant.

SUPERIOR COURT OF THE STATE OF _____

FOR THE COUNTY OF _____

|  |  |  |
|---|---|---|
| Plaintiff, ) | NO. | |
| ) | | |
| vs.                              ) | BILL OF PARTICULARS | |
| ) | | |
| ) | | |
| Defendant _____   ) | | |

|  |  |
|---|---|
| Cross-Complainant          ) | |
| ) | |
| vs.                             ) | |
| ) | |
| Cross-Defendant _____   ) | |

TO: CROSS-DEFENDANT, _____ AND TO HIS ATTORNEY OF RECORD:

NOTICE IS HEREBY GIVEN that the following show Cross-Complainant's demand in the Second, Third and Fourth Causes of Action of the Cross-Complaint for the recovery of which this action is brought, to-wit:

SECOND CAUSE OF ACTION

Attached hereto, marked Exhibit 1, is a copy of the account relating to the Second Cause of Action.

THIRD CAUSE OF ACTION

Attached hereto, marked Exhibit 2, is a copy of the account relating to the Third Cause of Action.

FOURTH CAUSE OF ACTION

The sum of $2,250.00 represents cash advances to Cross-Defendant. The sum of $250.00 rather than $350.00 as set forth in the Fourth Cause of Action of the Complaint, by typographical error, constitutes a travel advance.

DATED: March _____, 19___.

BY _____

Attorneys for Defendant and
Cross-Complainant.

## PLEADING ACTIONS IN EQUITY

### The Injunctive Process—General Procedure

1. The following injunctive process may be initiated and may occur prior to the actual trial of a case, with a full hearing on the merits of the claim.

(a) Prepare your complaint, in which is incorporated a request for temporary restraining order (commonly called TRO);

(b) Prepare a memorandum of points and authorities in support thereof;

(c) Prepare an affidavit or declaration of your attorney and/or client, or both;

(d) Prepare an order to show cause.

*Note*: The declarations must show irreparable harm or damage to the plaintiff, and the fact that the continuing negative action by defendant is not restrained by court order.

(e) As this is an ex-parte motion and order, prepare your ex-parte notice of motion.

(f) File the same with the court, in order to secure a date when the defendant must appear and show cause why the court should not issue a temporary restraining order enjoining him from continuing acts complained of.

### Defenses Which Can Be Pleaded to the Following Actions In Equity

Note that equity, as such, is abolished in the Federal Rules of Civil Procedure, and the state(s) that have adopted similar rules. However, the underlying equitable causes, still exist. Therefore, you are cautioned to check your local Court Rules to determine if this procedure is in effect, and if so, which rule is applicable.

A. *Specific Performance*

(1) Statute of Limitations (contracts must be in writing);

(2) Laches;

(3) Unclean hands;

(4) Hardship;

(5) Mistake and representations.

B. *Rescission*

(1) Election of remedies. You should discuss this defense with your attorney as it is a very tricky defense and must be treated with a great deal of clarity.

C. *Reformation*

(1) The defenses to reformation are the same as those for specific performance since there was a valid original contract.

D. *Declaratory Relief Actions*

(1) Here too, the defenses are the same as those listed above for specific performance.

## DEALING WITH STATUTES

### Introduction

If a plaintiff does not file his complaint within a certain time after a cause of action arises, it gives the defendant a defense which can defeat the plaintiff's cause of action and forever bar his claim of recovery. Consider the following checklist of statute dates which should be compared to your local state statutes to avoid a default based on the running of the statute applicable.

A. Answer—30 days; 20 days, Federal Rules of Civil Practice;

B. Service of Process—30 days; 20 days Federal Rules of Practice;

C. Answer to Unlawful Detainer action—10 to 30 days;

D. Personal Injury claim—1 year from date of accident;

E. Breach of Written Contract for Money—4 years;

F. Account Stated or Open Book Account—4 years;

G. Verbal contract—within 2 (3) years of the breach;

H. For trespass or injury to real property; or to recover personal property—2 to 4 years from date of occurrence;

I. Action for fraud or mistake—3 (4) years of date of discovery;

J. Tort actions, collection of damages, personal wrongs and money damages—within 1 year.

Separate and apart from the statute of limitations is the Rule of Laches. This merely means that the plaintiff delayed too long in filing his complaint and that his delay was unreasonable and prejudicial to the rights of the defendant. However, the apparent delay *must* appear on the face of the complaint, otherwise it would have to be raised as an issue within the complaint.

### COMPLAINT FOR FORECLOSURE OF
### AGREEMENT TO SALE

Attorney for Plaintiffs

SUPERIOR COURT OF _____, COUNTY OF _____

No.

Plaintiffs, )  C O M P L A I N T
)  FOR FORECLOSURE OF
vs.                    )  AGREEMENT OF SALE
)
)
)
Defendants. )
_____ )

Plaintiffs allege:

I

_____, a _____ corporation, is now and at all times herein mentioned was a corporation organized and existing under and by virtue of the laws of the State of _____, and authorized to do business and engage in business in the State of _____ with its offices located at

_____.

II

_____, a New Jersey corporation, is now and at all times herein mentioned was a corporation organized and existing under and by virtue of the laws of the State of New Jersey, and authorized to do and engage in business in the State of _____ with its offices located at _____.

### III

The true names or capacities, whether individual, corporate, associate, or otherwise, of defendants First Doe, Second Doe, and Third Doe are unknown to Plaintiff, who therefore sues said defendants by such fictitious names, and plaintiff will amend this complaint to show their true names and capacities when they are ascertained; each of said defendants has, or claims to have, some interest or claim on the property hereinafter described which interest or claim is subsequent to and subject to the claim of plaintiffs.

### IV

Plaintiffs are the owners of Lot _____, Tract _____, _____ and are entitled to possession of the same.

### V

Defendants on January 4, 19__ entered into an Agreement of Sale with Plaintiffs _____ and _____ for the purchase of Lot_____, Tract _____, _____ County at _____, for the sum of Forty-Nine Thousand and No/100 Dollars ($49,000), $1,500 of which was paid on the execution of the agreement, One Thousand ($1,000) of which was to be paid six (6) months from the date of possession or the close of escrow whichever is sooner, $1743.00 in six monthly installments of $290.50 each, with the balance of Forty-Six Thousand Five Hundred and No/100 ($46,500) Dollars due and payable on July 15, 19__, with the right of Buyers to obtain from Plaintiffs a loan secured by a second deed of trust for $7,300 of that amount. Defendants are required to pay all property taxes and any future special taxes or assessments which may be imposed during the term of the contract. A copy of the Agreement of Sale is attached as an Exhibit "A".

### VI

Defendants have failed to pay any of the amounts provided for in the Agreement of Sale other than paying the initial One Thousand Five Hundred Dollars ($1,500) at the time of execution of the Agreement of Sale.

### VII

It is provided in Paragraph "D" of the Agreement of Sale that:

"Buyer shall pay all property taxes and any future special taxes or assessments which may be imposed during the term of the Agreement."

### VIII

Defendants failed to pay their pro-rata share of the $697.67 real property taxes assessed by the County of _____ for the second installment of 19__ taxes and it was necessary for Plaintiffs to pay Defendants' share for Defendants' account. Defendants' share in 176/180 of $697.67 or $682.18. A copy of the letter making demand for payment of taxes is attached as an Exhibit "D".

### IX

It is provided in the FIFTH Condition of the Agreement of Sale that:

"Should the Buyer fail to make said payments or any thereof when due, or fail to comply with the conditions, covenants and agreements set forth herein, the amounts paid hereon may be retained by Seller as the consideration for making this agreement, and thereupon the Seller shall be released from all obligation in law or equity to convey said property, and any occupancy of said property thereafter by said Buyer shall be deemed to be, and be, a tenancy at the pleasure of the Seller. Buyer will immediately vacate the property upon written notice by the Seller, and Buyer shall never acquire, and expressly waives, any and all rights or claims of title because of such possession. Buyer acknowledges that the reasonable rental value of said property as of the date hereof is $490 per month."

Defendants as Buyers have failed to make the payments when due, the occupancy has been converted to a tenancy at the pleasure of Seller and Seller has made demand for payment of rent, which rent has not been paid.

### X

It is provided in the SIXTH Condition of the Agreement of Sale that:

"Should the Seller sue the Buyer to enforce this agreement of its terms, the Buyer shall pay a reasonable attorney's fee and all expenses in connection therewith."

It has become necessary by reason of the above mentioned defaults by defendants to employ an attorney at law duly licensed to practice in all of the courts of the State of _____, as its attorney to commence and prosecute this foreclosure action; the reasonable value of services of counsel in this action should be determined by the Court at the time of trial.

# Enforcing Judgments

*If you are in an office with a heavy collection practice, this is the chapter for you. All the step-by-step procedures you need; and all you want to know about the rights of the parties in this proceeding can be found here.*

# CHAPTER 15

## INTRODUCTION

The purpose of laws relating to proceedings in aid of execution of judgments is to create an economic and orderly procedure for the collection of debts, and to create priority of debt collection. In most states, this procedure is controlled by statute. Therefore, you are cautioned to check your local statutes before utilizing the hereinafter set forth tried and proven procedures—the reason being that these steps as set forth below are those followed under California law, and are merely an example of what you should look for and how to proceed.

## IN A NUTSHELL

1) Against what kind and type of properties may you enforce a judgment?

    a) All goods, chattels, money and property;

    b) Real and personal property or interest therein;

    c) Intangibles;

    d) Title without interest;

    e) Interest without title, and

    f) Joint interest.

2) What kind or portion of property is exempt from seizure?

   a) Necessities of life;
   b) Contingent interest;
   c) Estate at will;
   d) Choses in action not in writing, and
   e) Patents.

3) What supplemental aids are available for the discovery of such assets?

   a) Examination of judgment debtor;
   b) Examination of creditor of judgment debtor, and
   c) Special summary proceedings.

4) How may debtors attack creditors' efforts to enforce a judgment?

   a) Apply for stay of execution;
   b) File a motion to recall or quash;
   c) Claim an exemption;
   d) Apply to set aside an improper sale, and
   e) Redeem the property.

5) How may a third party or one claiming to have an interest in the property, attack the assets to enforce a judgment against a property?

   a) File an action to quiet title;
   b) File an undertaking to release the property;
   c) Demand or apply for a hearing on the matter;
   d) File the necessary legal documents to enjoin the sale or conversion and ask for damages.

6) What remedies are available to debtors and third persons for wrongful conduct on the part of a judgment creditor or some other person doing the collection process?

   a) File to enjoin or restrain the judgment of creditors;
   b) The judgment debtor can file a motion to quash the Writ;
   c) File on behalf of the judgment debtor a tort action for infliction of emotional distress; or invasion of privacy; or abuse of process; or slander; and/or trespass or conversion.

7) How do you enforce a judgment?

a) Obtain and secure issuance of a Writ of Execution and forward the same to the Sheriff for levy. (This may not be the procedure used in your state. Therefore, you are cautioned to check this procedure.)

8) To whom is it directed?

It is a notice to a third party in actual possession of property of the judgment debtor, to be held by said third party subject to attachment. For example, banks, employers and so forth.

## TIMESAVER HINTS

To avoid some of the typical problems you may encounter relative to executions against interest in land, note the following:

1) Be aware of the duration of the judgment lien, with the possibility of an extension or renewal;
2) Be sure of the proper method of enforcement, that is, whether by Writ of Execution or foreclosure proceedings;
3) Be cognizant of the types of money judgments capable of creating liens;
4) Take particular note of the types of interest in land covered thereby, such as titles, real, equitable interest, and property which was fraudulently conveyed;
5) Be on top of the extensions to "after acquired" property, and relative rank or priority of several liens;
6) Know the priorities and other effects resulting from judgment liens; and so forth. You might want to discuss other possible or projected problems with your attorney.

## PRE-HEARING STEP-BY-STEP PROCEDURE

After your attorney has completed the trial of an action involving a debt collection and an enforcement of a judgment to collect said monetary debt, you should prepare the following documents:

1. *Findings of fact:* this document relates all the facts heretofore stated in the case and presented to the court, and should have as a component part thereof the clause ''there are no further disputes as to the facts.''

2. *Conclusions of law:* (sometimes this document is a part of the findings of fact document and therefore would be called Findings of Fact and Conclusions of Law), which sets forth case authorities and law applicable to the case facts involved.

3. *Judgment:* this judgment can either be prepared by the clerk of the court for the judge's signature; or sometimes the judge in his order will direct that it be an ''attorney judgment,'' which therefore would be prepared by you as a legal assistant.

4. *Memorandum of costs:* which spells out the expenses incurred in the prosecution of the action, such as the court filing fees, jury fees, reporter fees and so forth. In most states this is a printed form, but it can be typed from scratch.

## STEP-BY-STEP PROCEDURE
## RE: EXAMINATION OF JUDGMENT DEBTOR

### I. Documents Prepared Before Examination:

1. An ex parte motion ordering debtor in;

2. An affidavit to be signed by your attorney which is being filed on behalf of the judgment creditor; or

3. An affidavit prepared for the signature of the judgment creditor. In any and all events, the following terminology should be included in any such affidavit:

    a) A statement of facts showing that the judgment was obtained, which would include the court of jurisdiction, the county and city wherein the case is heard, and the names of the plaintiff and defendant, together with the case number;

    b) There should be a concise statement that the judgment has in no way been satisfied, vacated or reversed, and most important, that it has not been barred by the statute of limitations;

    c) That the judgment debtor resides or has a place of business in the county, or is otherwise located within 150 miles of the place of examination (you are cautioned to check the local applicable mileage in your state).

4. Another document to be prepared prior to an examination would be the order for the signature of the judge who would hear the examination.

5. If you want the debtor to produce certain documents at the hearing, you should prepare a subpoena duces tecum and attach the same to the affidavit heretofore prepared. You are therefore cautioned to spell out, with specificity and clarity, descriptions of the documents, checks, receipts, etc. that you want the debtor to bring to the examination.

6. Where the basis of an order is a refusal on the part of a judgment debtor to supply a list of certain assets, then the affidavit heretofore described should include the following:

    (a) That the judgment debtor is known to have the assets described;

    (b) That the judgment creditor has made a demand for a list of such assets; and

    (c) That the facts of the case give rise to the likelihood that the judgment debtor will abscond with the property so described.

## II. Documents to Be Prepared After Examination of Judgment Debtor

1. An order for non-exempt property;

2. A memorandum of costs to be filed with the court, as hereinabove described; and

3. Prepare a Writ of Execution or other applicable document in your state to attach the debtor's salary, bank account, car, yacht, to place a lien on the debtor's house; and, of course, prepare and file your Abstract of Judgment.

## III. Documents Which May Be Prepared in a Contempt Proceeding for Failure on the Part of the Judgment Debtor to Conform to the Order Issued by the Court

1. An affidavit which sets forth the failure of a debtor to comply with the judgment; that the debtor disobeyed an order for examination; that

the debtor has removed assets from the jurisdiction of the court; and failure of the judgment debtor to deliver the assets to the judgment creditor, as ordered by the court.

You should also include, if applicable, that the judgment debtor had the ability to comply with the order; that the judgment debtor had a copy of the order, and that the judgment debtor willfully disobeyed said order.

*Timesaver:* Always attach an Order to your Affidavit for the benefit of the judge hearing the matter.

## STEP-BY-STEP PROCEDURE
## RE: ENFORCING JUDGMENT IN OTHER STATES

Although the following procedure for collection of judgments in sister states is applicable to California, the same type of procedure is utilized in your state, and you are therefore cautioned to check the appropriate Code of Civil Procedure and section in your state that covers sister state money judgments.

The application which must be executed under oath, should include the following:

1. A statement that an action in this state on a sister judgment state is not barred by the applicable statute of limitations;

2. A statement based on the applicant's information and belief that no stay of enforcement of the sister state judgment is currently in effect in the sister state;

3. A statement that the amount remains unpaid under the sister state judgment;

4. A statement that no action based on the sister state judgment is currently pending in any court in your state, and that no judgment based on the sister state judgment has previously been entered in any proceeding in the state;

5. Where the judgment debtor is an individual, a statement setting forth the name and last known resident address of the judgment debtor should be set forth, except for facts which are matters of public record in the state. The statement required by this particular paragraph may be made on the basis of a judgment creditor's information and belief, and, finally:

6. A statement setting forth the name and address of the judgment creditor.

It is important, and a prime prerequisite, that a properly authenticated copy of the sister state judgment accompany and be attached to the aforementioned application.


## STEP-BY-STEP PROCEDURE FOR EXECUTION

### 1. Issuance of Writ (of Mandamus).

a. Application and time of issuance of writ has a statutory limitation: you should check your local codes to determine this period. In California, it is ten years at the entry of judgment, at the discretion of the court; and the application may be made by the judgment creditor or his personal representative if the judgment creditor should die.


### 2. Levy on Property.

a. The duty and liability of a levying officer.

(i) The officer must levy on a sufficient amount of property to satisfy the judgment. When and if the property is more than the judgment, he should levy only on that part of the property which would satisfy the judgment creditor and at the discretion of the judgment debtor. The judgment debtor has the right to indicate which property may be levied upon to satisfy the judgment plus costs.

b. Time of levy and return.

(i) Once again you have a statutory limitation within which to levy and return. At least this is the procedure in the State of California and you should also check your local code with reference to this returnable date. In California, however, it's a returnable date of 60 days and may be withdrawn at the discretion of the levying officer to avoid the interruption of a pending sale.


### 3. Sale.

a. Duty to sell.

(i) The purpose of the levy is to sell the property to satisfy the judgment. This the levying officer must do.

(ii) The excess of proceeds of any such sale is returnable to the judgment debtor.

b. Notice requirement.

(i) As it relates to perishable goods or material, the posted notices of time and place of sale should be done in three places in the city or judicial district—within reason.

(ii) Other personal property should be posted in three places not less than ten days from the date of the sale; and personal notice must be mailed or delivered within not less than ten days.

(iii) Real property or leasehold: Here a notice must be posted publicly and on the property not less than ten days from the date of sale; publication should be accomplished once a week for that same 20 day period in a paper of general circulation;

(iv) Any person, in writing, may request written notice of the sale.

c. Conduct of sale.

The following is true generally—

(i) It may be conducted in the county.

(ii) It may be conducted at auction.

(iii) It may be conducted to the highest bidder or only enough may be sold to satisfy the judgment.

(iv) The debtor, if present, may direct the order in which the property, real or personal, shall be sold when the property consists of lots or parcels or of articles which can be sold to his advantage if sold separately.

All of the above may be peculiar to California only and the conduct of sale of property under such a writ may vary from state to state. Hence, you are once again cautioned to check your local codes for this procedure.

It should be noted, relative to the sale and conduct of the sale of property in connection with the satisfaction of a judgment where there are several known lots or parcels of real property and they are sold separately, that departure from this procedure is merely an irregularity and not grounds for setting aside the sale unless actual injury by this departure is shown. Further, in connection with the sale of real property, payment must be made in cash in full, together with all costs involved in connection with the relief of a judgment. In addition, property capable of manual delivery is delivered by the sheriff who provides the purchaser with a certificate of sale which in the case of realty may be recorded.

## RIGHTS AND REMEDIES OF JUDGMENT DEBTOR

1. Stay of Execution

    a. If the judgment debtor appeals, he may obtain a stay. To do this, a bond is required unless the court, in its discretion, rules otherwise. (Check your local code of procedure to determine this ruling.)

2. A motion can be prepared to recall or quash the execution.

    a. The court has inherent power to control its own process and may recall or quash a writ which was improperly or inadvertently issued. (Check your code of procedure for this ruling.) The basis of a court's ability to recall or quash such a writ may be the following:

        (i)   The decree may not have been a money judgment;

        (ii)  The judgment may have been subject to partial offset of the judgment;

        (iii) Or the judgment may have been heretofore satisfied.

    b. The Step-by-step procedure for recalling or quashing of a judgment:

        (i)   A noticed motion must be prepared;

        (ii)  If the writ is not void on its face only a party to the action may make the motion;

        (iii) Appealable order-grounds;
             1. Levy upon exempted property
             2. Not a money judgment,
             3. Abuse of process,
             4. Malicious prosecution.

        (iv)  An order to quash the levy is also appropriate (in public property not subject to execution) where the levy is upon exempt property. You should check your code of procedure and follow the ruling applicable in your state.

3. Claim of Exemption

The code of procedure controls these claims and unless otherwise provided, exemption is waived unless claimed. Your local code of procedure sets forth and delineates these exemptions.

*Note*: Injuctive relief has been granted against successive levies of exempt property.

4. Setting Aside Improper Sale

a. This may be accomplished either by a motion or by an independent action in equity. To justify this remedy, the judgment debtor would have to show serious prejudice to his interests, and minor procedural irregularities will not suffice. That is to say, mere inadequacy of price without proof of fraud, or other unfairness, will not be sufficient. The price itself may be a significant factor in showing unfairness even though strict fraud is not shown.

b. If the judgment debtor takes an appeal and has not stayed execution, a sale may occur and unless the purchaser is a bona fide purchaser, the sale may be set aside or restitution ordered upon the success of the appeal. (*Note:* Wrongful sale may give rise to twin actions.)

5. Redemption within 12 months (this statutory limitation may be different in your state).

Persons entitled to this right of redemption may be as follows:

a. Judgment debtor or his successor in interest;

b. Redemptioner, subsequent lien holder (may be in a lien holder not only a judgment creditor as it relates to a mortgage). The procedure for redeeming property is generally as follows: payment should be made to the last redemptioner including any previous liens; notification to the sheriff; and recording the notice of redemption.

## CHECKLIST RE JUDGMENTS

### A. Judgment Enforceable by Execution

1. Must be final and unconditional.
2. It must be sufficiently certain in form to constitute an enforceable personal judgment for money.
3. It must be a valid and subsisting obligation.
4. It must be a money judgment.

### B. Property Subject to Execution

Check your local code regarding this jurisdiction. The California Code of Civil Procedure is stated here by way of example):

1. The California Code states that all goods, chattels, money or other property, both real and personal, or any interest therein, of a judgment-debtor not exempt by law are liable to execution.

2. Interest of Judgment Debtor.

a) Title without interest. The creditor can acquire no greater interest than his debtor, if debtor only has a parent title with no interest. The execution creditor under these conditions would get nothing;

b) Interest without title. When the debtor makes a fraudulent conveyance, his creditors may execute directly on the property in the hands of the transferor which would be the purchaser.

3. Joint Interests. Joint tenancy interest may be executed upon.

4. Equitable Interests. A ''vested equitable interest'' may be executed upon. The vested equitable interest of a beneficiary of trusts (watch for spendthrift clauses, however), as well as equitable converted interests of contract land purchases.

5. Property subject to security interest may be executed upon in order that the third party may protect himself under special statutory proceedings.

*Note*: Check your local codes for this special proceeding.

6. Property rights not subject to levy, such as:

   i) contingent interest
   ii) privileges of licenses,
   iii) an estate at will
   iv) patent rights and trademarks; and,
   v) choses in action not represented in writing.

7. Cause of action. The California Code of Procedure provides for the court in which an action is pending to grant a lien, or allow intervention upon the cause of action.

*Note*: You might wish to check the Federal Rules of Civil Procedure, Supp. Rule C(5); Supp. Rule E(5)(a,b); as well as your local court and code regulations governing the above and foregoing.

## CHECKLIST FOR PRIORITIES

(You are once again cautioned to check your local code of civil procedure as to these priorities. The California Code of Procedure is being used by way of example.)

A) Priorities depend upon the statutes granting them, but more importantly upon when a lien arises. In California, the code provides that an execution will have no effect upon property until the time that the levy and liens normally begin. However, when there is an attachment of judgment lien, the title of execution purchaser relates back to the time of commencement of earlier liens.

To create a judgment lien, you must have a money judgment; a judgment must have been duly entered according to your local code requirements; and there must be a recordation of abstract of judgment with the county recorder of each county where the real property is located. Judgment liens have priority according to the date the lien arises. The lien arises as follows:

1. By virtue of the rendition of a judgment;
2. An entry and filing of abstract of judgment with the county recorder where the judgment debtor has property;
3. Or after acquired, then the lien arises when the property is acquired.

A) The lien arises as the result of an execution; or arises at the time of a levy, which is the practice in California.

B) Priorities are also affected by the duration of the judgment lien. That could be, for example, ten years from the date of entry unless, as in some states, the same is stayed upon appeal.

C) Priorities are also affected by the execution of a lien. That is to say, how the same was created, for example, by levy. Here again, priorities of an execution lien are determined by the duration, that is to say, it could be one year from the date; thereafter an alias execution would be necessary.

D) Then you have your priorities as between execution creditors which are dependent upon, as in California, the first to levy; to a priority lienholder if his lien is valid.

(You should follow your statutory requirements in this regard as the law states that a prior lienholder prevails over the execution creditor.)

E) A prior grantee under an unrecorded deed prevails over the execution creditor since the latter is not a bona fide purchaser unless the execution creditor becomes a bona fide purchaser at the execution sale.

In California, that recordation must be perfected according to statutory prerequisities. This is a matter of law and you are once again cautioned to check your local code as it relates to the recordation of deeds and priorities.

# Handling the Criminal Case

# CHAPTER 16

*Every legal assistant should be able to name, know and have a working knowledge of all the steps involved in a criminal procedure in his state. Every legal assistant should know the motions commonly used in pre-trial and post-trial procedures, as well as the writs pertinent.*

## INTRODUCTION

As the legal assistant in the office, you should not only be familiar with the classification and types of clients, but also the various facets of criminal practice. You should have a thorough working knowledge of what pre-trial, as opposed to post-trial, motion should be prepared for the benefit of your employer-attorney. You should also be able to conduct an in-depth initial interview with the accused, and to determine what documents should be prepared in preparation for the defense of a case by your employer-attorney.

## INTERVIEWING THE ACCUSED

Here, more than in any other phase of law practice, your attitude toward and treatment of a client should be professional. Remember, though there will be times when you will be appalled at the alleged crime; or not in sympathy with the alleged act of violence, and the like, you are not there to sit in judgment, but you are there to help the client. Bear this in mind and consider the following when interviewing such an individual.

## 1. Basic Questions to Ask

A. Obtain a detailed statement of the facts surrounding the alleged crime;

B. What the client did as it related to the alleged crime;

C. How the alleged crime really occurred;

D. If the client recalls any witnesses being present, and if so, their names and addresses, and any other identifying information as to these individuals.

## 2. Pertinent Questions to Ask About the Client

A. Personal history, including marital status, health, finances, education, work experience, occupation, hobbies;

B. Any prior record of violence;

C. Any prior felony convictions;

D. Whom you can obtain as a character witness; credibility;

E. Whom to call to aid in obtaining money for bond;

F. Did he commit the crime with which he was charged?

## Step-by-Step Procedures: Arrest to Trial to Appeal

A. *Pre-Trial Procedure:*

1. The defendant appears in court for the arraignment to enter a plea;

2. He may plead guilty and have the matter set for sentencing; or he may plead not guilty and have the matter set for trial;

3. When a felony is charged against a defendant, the procedure may be as follows:

(a) After arrest, defendant may be arraigned within a specific time period, and assuming a guilty plea is not entered, the court may set the matter for a preliminary hearing;

(b) If, after the preliminary hearing, the court decides that sufficient cause exists to hold defendant for trial, the client may then be rearraigned in another court and the matter set for trial.

B. *Pre-Trial Motions Which May Be Prepared:*

1. Motion to reduce bail;

2. Motion to squash or set aside complaint or indictment;

3. Motion to dismiss;

4. Motion for change of venue;

5. Motion for discovery;

6. Motion to suppress evidence;

7. Motion to sever;

8. Motion for appointment of an expert.

C. *Jury Selection*—Your role in this phase of the trial would be as follows:

1. Obtaining the areas of residence from local Board of Registrations, Tax Assessor's Office, Dept. of Motor Vehicles, etc.;

2. Checking political and organizational affiliations;

3. Checking the nature of any petitions signed and determining if they have any children or animals or unusual hobbies, and so forth.

D. *The Trial:*

In preparing your attorney for trial, you should:

1. Coordinate the activities pertinent to the trial;

2. Interview and locate witnesses;

3. Set up deposition of witnesses;

4. Prepare witnesses for examination and cross-examination;

5. Prepare the necessary exhibits; and

6. Prepare the trial brief, which should include the following:

(a) A police report;

(b) Profile of the witnesses and their testimony;

(c) Investigation file; and

(d) A research memorandum.

E. *Prepare Your Jury Instructions.* This is one of your more crucial duties in trial preparation. You should discuss these thoroughly with your attorney.

F. *Prepare the Draft for the Opening and Final Arguments of Your Attorney.* The following guide should be considered:

1. Outline both the prosecution and defense case; and

2. Note the items of evidence which have been introduced and which of these, if any, would be most helpful to your attorney's argument;

3. Then develop a legal memorandum accordingly.

G. *Post-Trial Procedures:*

1. Prepare a Motion for New Trial;

2. Prepare Application for Probation, and/or

3. File a Notice of Appeal.

(a) Prepare Request for Record on Appeal, which includes the Clerk's Transcript (record during trial), the Reporter's Transcript, copies of all motions filed and jury instructions.

4. Petition for Re-Hearing or Review;

5. It should be noted that recourse to the appellate courts may be had by way of the following motions:

(a) Writ of Habeas Corpus;

(b) Writ of Prohibition;

(c) Writ of Mandate.

## DEFINITIVE STEP-BY-STEP PROCEDURES POST-TRIAL TO APPEAL

A. After the verdict has been rendered, file a motion for new trial (if applicable), the exception being the preparation and filing of a motion for reduction of bail, if the same is excessive.

B. Then, interview the jurors after the trial to determine how they reached their verdict.

C. If your motion for a new trial is denied and the client is sent to jail, recall that he can be given either (a) state probation or (b) probation conditioned upon service of time in the county jail (both of which are dependent upon local statute and criminal procedure).

To enhance your value to your attorney as a legal assistant, be aware that even after the conviction, there is a great deal that you can do to prepare the defendant for the imposition of the probation department.

Consider the following:

1. The legal assistant can interview the defendant as to convictions, prior offenses, employment history and the like.

2. The legal assistant can also delve into areas which could mitigate punishment and/or reduce the sentence, such as a feeling of remorse and penitence on the part of the defendant;

3. or can determine the need or possible desire for psychiatric examination or treatment for the defendant; and of course,

4. job rehabilitation.

5. On the date of the probation and sentence hearing, you should file your notice of appeal. (This form is similar in format to that of a civil appeal). (In California, this right to appeal is statutory if the defendant has not pleaded guilty.) Further, it usually takes about 80 days. You are cautioned to check your local codes for this time restriction.

6. At the time of filing the notice of appeal, request the preparation of the record on appeal which consists of the following:

    A. Clerk's transcript.
    B. The reporter's transcript.
    C. Any pretrial motions.
    D. Closing arguments.
    E. Voir Dire questions to the jury.
    F. Arguments as to the jury instructions.

7. Thirty days after the receipt of the above record on appeal (or other applicable statutory period of time), the appellant files an opening brief which may consist of the following:

    A. Statement of the proceedings in the case;
    B. Statement of the facts taken from the record on appeal which support your attorney's argument.
    C. Point or points of law which the appellant contends should require the appeal judge to reverse the verdict, such as, improper jury instructions, search and seizure items admitted into evidence, and the like.

8. The respondent (attorney general) thereafter has 30 days or other appropriate statutory period, from the filing of the opening brief, within which to file a reply brief.

9. Thereafter, your attorney may file a reply brief to the attorney general's reply brief.

*Note*: The foregoing is optional. As a practical matter, however, it is always done since the defendant has a heavier burden of proof after conviction and it is incumbent upon him to rebut the substantial evidence contained in the attorney general's reply brief.

10. After all brief arguments are in, oral arguments are scheduled and are normally heard in the district court where the appeal was filed. Your office is notified by the court when a decision has been made, either reversing or affirming the verdict.

11. Thereafter, you have 15 days within which to file a petition for rehearing.

12. After the appeals court decision is filed, you have a 40-day maximum in which to file a petition in the supreme court. (Note that all of these statutory limitations should be checked against your local codes since they may vary from jurisdiction to jurisdiction.

*Cautionary Measure:* As a result of the foregoing, you should be aware of writs which can be filed in connection with the above appellate review, such as a Writ of Mandamus or Writ of Certiorari.

For your review, recall that a Writ of Mandamus is either peremptory or alternative, according to whether it requires the defendant absolutely to obey its behest, or gives him an opportunity to show cause to the contrary. It is the usual practice to issue the alternative writ first. This commands the defendants to do the particular act, or else to appear and show cause against it at a day and time certain. If the defendant neglects to obey the writ, and either defaults in his appearance or fails to show good cause against the application, the peremptory Mandamus issues, which commands him absolutely and without qualification to do the act.

The act of Mandamus is one, brought in a Court of competent jurisdiction, to obtain an Order of such Court commanding an inferior court, tribunal, board, corporation, or person, to do or not to do an act, the performance or omission of which the law enjoins as a duty resulting from an office, trust, or station.

And, a Writ of Certiorari is an appellate proceeding for re-examination of actions of inferior tribunals, or an auxiliary process to enable the appellate court to obtain further information in a pending cause. It brings into superior court the record of the administrative or inferior judicial tribunal for inspection; to correct errors of law, such as erroneous or unwanted acts or proceedings.[1]

## INTRODUCTION TO FORMS

Consider the following forms as a guide to any form you might be preparing on behalf of the defendant in a criminal case. Note those items which are underscored, since they are pertinent to the defense of your client and

---

[1] The definitions of these Writs were obtained from *Black's Law Dictionary*, Revised Fourth Edition, West Publishing Company, St. Paul, Minnesota.

mandatory to the contents of any pleading being filed on behalf of a criminal defendant. Be aware that any document prepared on behalf of a defendant in a criminal law matter must be drafted with particularity and the information set forth therein spelled out with specificity and clarity.

### NOTICE OF MOTION FOR SUPPRESSION OF EVIDENCE

(Name) _____
(Address) _____
(Telephone Number) _____

Attorney for Defendant John Doe

SUPERIOR COURT OF THE STATE OF _____
FOR THE COUNTY OF _____

THE PEOPLE OF THE STATE
OF _____,                No. _____
                 Plaintiff, )
                            )
     vs.                    )
                            )
                            )     NOTICE OF MOTION FOR
     JOHN DOE,              )     SUPPRESSION OF EVIDENCE
               Defendant. )     (Pen. Code §)
     _____ )

NOTICE IS HEREBY GIVEN THAT ON JANUARY 21, 19__, at 11:00 a.m. or as soon thereafter as counsel may be heard, in the Courtroom of Division _____ of the above-entitled court, located at _____ in the City of _____, defendant, JOHN DOE, will move the court for an order suppressing as evidence the following: All property taken on December 18, 19__ from those certain premises located at _____, _____, at the time of the defendant's arrest at said time and place, consisting of the wooden crate, containing ten empty bottles, a pile of rags, two cans of gasoline, two incendiary devices, and four kilos of marijuana; together with all evidence respecting any events that occurred at said time and place and all fruits thereof.

## NOTICE OF MOTION RE: INFORMATION

(Name) _____

(Address) _____

(Telephone No.) _____

Attorney for Defendant

SUPERIOR COURT OF THE STATE OF _____

FOR THE COUNTY OF _____

THE PEOPLE OF THE STATE     CASE NO. 234 567
OF _____,
                    Plaintiff, )     NOTICE OF MOTION
                               )     RE: Information
                 v.            )        (Section 995)
JANE DOE,                      )        Penal Code.)
                 Defendant.    )
_____        )

    TO _____, DISTRICT ATTORNEY OF _____
COUNTY, _____:
    PLEASE TAKE NOTICE that on _____, 19__, at _____
A.M., or as soon thereafter as counsel can be heard, in Department _____ of the
above-entitled court, located at _____, _____,
_____, defendant JANE DOE will move the court for an order *setting
aside the information* filed herein.
    Said motion will be made on the grounds that _____, in that
_____, as shown on pages _____, lines _____ of the transcript of
the preliminary examination.
    Said motion will be based on this notice of motion, on the transcript of the
preliminary examination, on the attached declaration of _____, and
the Memorandum of Points and Authorities served herewith, and on such other
oral and documentary evidence as may be presented at the hearing on this motion.
    Dated: _____

_____
                              Attorney for Defendant
(*Note:* A similar form may be used in connection with an indictment, if and where
         applicable.)

## PETITION FOR WRIT OF HABEAS CORPUS

(Name) _____
(Address) _____
(Telephone Number) _____

SUPREME COURT OF THE STATE OF _____

| | | |
|---|---|---|
| _____, on | ) | No. _____ |
| behalf of John Doe, | ) | |
| | ) | PETITION FOR WRIT OF |
| Petitioner, | ) | HABEAS CORPUS |
| vs. | ) | |
| | ) | NAME OF PERSON IN |
| _____, Sheriff of | ) | CUSTODY: JOHN DOE |
| _____, SUPERIOR COURT | | |
| OF STATE OF _____ | ) | RELATIONSHIP OF PETI- |
| FOR THE COUNTY | ) | TIONER TO PERSON IN |
| OF _____, | ) | CUSTODY: ATTORNEY |
| | ) | |
| DEPARTMENT _____, | ) | |
| Respondents. | ) | |
| _____ | ) | |

TO THE HONORABLE _____ AND TO THE ASSOCIATE JUSTICES OF THE SUPREME COURT OF THE STATE OF _____.

1. John Doe in whose behalf the writ is applied for is confined or restrained of his liberty at the ____County Jail by Sheriff _____ and the Superior Court of the State of _____ for the County of _____.

2. Name and location of court under whose process person is confined: Superior Court of the State of _____ for the County of _____.

3. Nature of court proceeding (e.g., criminal case, commitment for narcotics addition, insanity, or mentally disordered.

This motion will be made on the grounds that the search and seizure were pursuant to a warrant and unreasonable because there was no probable cause for the issuance of the warrant and the method of execution violated both federal and state constitutional standards.

Said motion will be based on the Declaration of Jane Doe and the ....

PETITION FOR WRIT OF MANDAMUS

Attorney Information

IN THE
UNITED STATES DISTRICT COURT
FOR THE EASTERN DISTRICT OF _____

Inmate's Name, Civil Action No.

          Petitioner,   )
                    )
  vs.               )         PETITION FOR WRIT OF
                    )         MANDAMUS (60 days Show Cause)
                    )
_____,   )        (Key Phrases)
Warden, et al.,
UNITED STATES PENITENTIARY,
MARION, _____,)
                    )
         Respondent. )
_____ )

TO: THE HONORABLE _____
GREETINGS:
    COMES NOW THE PETITIONER, above-named, to move this Honorable Court for relief from oppressive action by the above-named Respondent, action that has deprived this Petitioner of fundamental Constitutional Rights and which were in direct violation of recent Supreme Court Rulings, which will hereinafter be more fully shown.

    JURISIDICTION

    JURISIDCTION IS VESTED IN THIS COURT BY VIRTUE OF 28 U.S.C., Sections 1343; 1361; 1391(e); 1651; 1654; 2201; 2241; 2243. 42 U.S.C. Sections 1983 and 1985. Rule 8(a)(1), 3.

.....

    ARGUMENT

    A plaintiff is never required to exhaust administrative remedies when to do so would be obviously futile. This is especially true in Civil Rights cases where the Congressional Policy of providing a federal form for vindication of constitutional rights is particularly strong. ....

    A person does not lose all of his constitutional rights upon entering prison. *Betha v. Crouse,* 417 F.2d 504 (C.A. Id. 1969), and this is especially true of his rights under the First Amendment. See *Dennis v. United States,* 341 U.S. 494 (1951), wherein the court said:

> "...(in the area of the First Amendment freedoms)...we have pointed out that stringent standards are to be applied to the governmental restrictions...and rigid scrutiny must be brought to bear on the justification for encroachment on such rights."

. . . .

## SUMMATION

The Respondent Warden _____ is fully responsible for the conduct and actions of his underlings and it is his duty to uphold the Constitutional Rights of his prisoner wards, but rather than attempt to place any form of control on his subordinates and uphold the Constitution and Rules of the Supreme Court, Mr. _____ runs a haphazard institution, allowing employees to operate autonomously and without regard for the law, the rules of the United States Supreme Court or the constitutional rights of prisoners; or the public at large. For these reasons, the writ should issue and the release sought to be granted forthwith.

## RELEASE SOUGHT

THAT THIS HONORABLE COURT ENJOIN THE HEREIN NAMED RE-SPONDENT TO:

1. Remove the restrictions placed upon this prisoner's First Amendment rights to correspond;

2. Restore the thirty (30) days forfeited by the institution's disciplinary committee;

3. Deliver all correspondence, legal material and law books to this petitioner without any form of delay or censorship;

4. Award compensation for punitive damages due to mental anguish and frustration suffered by this petitioner;

5. Give any other such just and equitable relief as the court may deem warranted by facts which appear herein.

## CONCLUSION

The petitioner in this cause of action is a layman, unrepresented prisoner seeking relief as best he knows how without the aid of qualified counsel, therefore, may the Court be respectfully reminded of such cases as *French v. Hayne,* 547 F.2d 994 (C.A. 7 1976); *Haynes v. Kerner,* 404 U.S. 519 (1972); *Carmelly v. Gibson,* 335 U.S. 41, 45-6 (1957), wherein it has been clearly determined that if an unrepresented prisoner seeks an inappropriate type of relief, they, the courts, will interpret the complaint as seeking whatever type of relief as is warranted by the facts of the case.

. . . .

In accordance with 28 U.S.C., Section 1746(2), I declare under the penalty of perjury, that the foregoing is true and correct to the best of my knowledge and belief.

Executed on this _____ day of _____, 19__.

_____
INMATE,
Petitioner Pro Se

*Note:* (The above and foregoing writ of mandamus was prepared in pro per by inmate, _____).

# CHAPTER 17

# Working with Copyright Registrations and Trademarks

*This chapter concerns itself with the highly specialized field of unfair business practices. Its contents will give you all you need to know to become knowledgeable and adept in preparing any documentation assigned by your attorney.*

As you know, as of January 1, 1978, there were many changes made in the application forms for copyrights as well as in their content and format.

## THINGS TO REMEMBER

1. Form TX is for published and unpublished non-dramatic literary works;

2. Form PA is a form for published and unpublished works for musicians, dramatic works, pantomimes and choreography; as well as for motion pictures and other audio-visual manuscripts;

3. Form DA is to be used for visual works such as graphics, sculpture, etc.;

4. Form SR is for published and unpublished recordings;

5. Form RE is for the removal of copyrights, which have heretofore been copyrighted under the old law.

## Special Problems

6. Form CA is for a supplemental registration to correct or augment information already submitted to the copyright office;

7. Form GR/CP is an adjunct application which is used for the registration of a group of contributors to periodicals; and

8. Form IS is used when requesting issuance of an import statement under the manufacturing provisions of a copyright law.

## Special Statutory Periods

Copyright applications secured between 1950 and 1977 must be renewed. They expire at the end of their 28th calendar year.

Copyright applications in their second term on January 1, 1978, are automatically extended up to a period of 75 years without the need for renewal.

Works already in the public domain cannot be protected under this new law.

The copyright act has no procedure for restoring protection for works where the copyright has been lost for any reason.

## Costs of Registering Copyright Claims*

1. For each registration, $10.
2. For each renewal, $6.
3. Basic fee for recordation of a statement revealing the identity of the author of an anonymous work, $10.
4. Additional pages or title, $1.

## Costs of Recording Documents, Which Include Certification

1. Basic fee, $10.
2. Additional pages or title, $50.

## TRADEMARKS

Two basic approaches to trademark infringements are:

1) You can file a complaint and sue for money damages incurred;

---

*Dollars figures as of publication date.

or 2) you can file a complaint for injunctive relief in a court of equity.

Recall that the basic elements of infringement are as follows:

(a) When one uses a mark which is identical to, or

(b) Is confusingly similar to a registered trademark; and

(c) Where the plaintiff's mark or name is referred to a "weak name."

The test, remember, is whether there is a liklihood of confusion on the part of the consuming public as to the actual source of the product purchased.

A weak name is one which is commonly used, and although associated with plaintiff's product or service, is associated with many others, such as, "Time Magazine," "time" being the weak name.

*Cautionary Measure:* Be aware that no fraudulent intent is required to constitute a trademark infringement, only the "likelihood of confusion."

Oftentimes, you will be delegated the responsibility to develop legal research and set forth the distinction of trademarks and trade names prior to the filing of a law suit to protect the interests of a client. To this end, consider the following step-by-step procedures, and the following factors in determining the likelihood of confusion.

I. Determine the degree of similarity between the mark of the plaintiff and the mark of the defendant as to the appearance, pronunciation or verbal translation; or even, suggestion of the name;

II. Determine the relation of the use and the manner of the marketing of a product or service as between the plaintiff and defendant;

III. Determine whether or not it is more likely to be noticed or purchased by an expert buyer than by a lay consumer. That is, one with a fair knowledge of the art or product, as opposed to the other who has no such expertise;

IV. Determine the intent of the alleged infringer.

*Remember:* Traditionally, the trademark was considered a copyright, and hence, infringement would be a trespass. On the other hand, a trademark was never viewed as a property right.

Today, it is not necessary to show fraudulent intent in either trademark or trade name infringement. The remedy as to both is in law for money damages or in a court of equity for injunctive relief.

## TRADE NAMES (BASIC ELEMENTS)

There are no limitations (such as generic, personal or geographical) on what may be used as a trade name. All of those designations, which would otherwise fail as a protectable trademark, may qualify as a protectable trade name. The key here is "the acquisition of a secondary meaning."

Second meaning, as heretofore discussed, is nothing more than "an earned reputation," which indicates that the words no longer have a "special meaning," but rather, that the public has attached to it a meaning which identifies a product or service as coming from a particular source.

Hence, a trade name may be any designation which is used to identify goods or services of a merchant or manufacturer, *and through its association with the goods or services,* has acquired a secondary meaning.

Though the secondary meaning as it relates to a trade name may be protected, you should be aware that it is not so easy to establish the "secondary meaning"—it is therefore more incumbent upon you to cause the registration of the trademark and if, as a fringe benefit it becomes a trade name, all well and good for the client.

### Suggested Defenses to the Infringement of a Trade Name

1. Unclean hands;
2. Laches;
3. Torts of trademark and trade name infringement;
4. Consent;
5. Abandonment (or non-use), and
6. The trademark becoming a generic name.

## TRADE SECRETS

Factors which the court will consider in determining protective or trade secrets, and which you should therefore include in any complaint being filed in connection with the protection of a trade secret, are as follows:

1. The expediture of money, time and labor in developing the trade secret;
2. The novelty of the secret;

3. Whether or not it is, in fact, a secret;

4. The conscientious and continuing effort on the part of the owner to keep and/or maintain this secret;

5. The value of the secret to the business entity;

6. The extent to which it is, was, and/or may be isolated; and

7. The relationship between the parties having knowledge of the secret, i.e., employee-employer.

## For Your Information

Generally, a trade secret is protected as follows, and you should be aware of this when interviewing and/or preparing your complaint from notes in the files from your attorney:

1) As between employer-employee a written agreement; though we have experienced that often the employer will protect his secret in a verbal manner, but this is ill-advised;

2) By way of an implied promise on the part of the employee to the employer that he or she would not divulge the secret of his operations.

## ELEMENTS TO INCLUDE IN A COMPLAINT FOR UNFAIR (COMPETITION INJUNCTIVE RELIEF) BASED ON A "TRADE SECRET"

The following elements *must be present* before you, as a legal assistant, can draft a complaint which will sustain a good, valid cause of action in an unfair competition lawsuit:

1. You must be able to show that the plaintiff was harmed;

2. That the plaintiff used every acceptable and reasonable means to protect his "trade secret";

3. That the defendant had fiduciary knowledge of the "trade secret" and access thereto;

4. That the defendant converted the same for his own use and benefit;

5. That the defendant in using and converting plaintiff's trade secret intended to mislead and defraud the public;

6. That the defendant, in doing the acts above referred to, violated the fiduciary relationship as between employee and employer;

7. That the "secret", illegally converted by the defendant, was not of a nature of the type of secret which could be legitimately retained in the mind of a defendant and therefore, could be legally used by said defendant for his own use and benefit.

The documents which should accompany a complaint for unfair competition are as follows:

1. Notice of Motion for Preliminary Injunction;
2. Memorandum of Points and Authorities in Support of said Motion;
3. Declaration of your attorney (and if so advised), Declaration or Affidavit by the client and/or plaintiff.

## DEFINITION/COMPARISON CHECKLIST

1. *Trade Secret*—A trade secret is a plan or process, tool, mechanism or compound; formula or process not patented, but known only to certain individuals and its owner, and those of his employees in whom it may be necessary to confide.

2. *Trademark*—A trademark is any work, name, symbol, or device or any combination thereof, adopted and used by a manufacturer or merchant to identify his goods and distinguish them from those manufactured or sold by others.

OR

A *TRADEMARK* is any mark, letter, or word (and the like) used to identify and distinguish goods of a particular person. The primary intent of a trademark is to protect—to prevent the confusion of the consuming public. IT MUST BE AFFIXED TO THE GOODS IN A COMMERCIAL SENSE.

3. *Service mark*—A service mark is used in the sale or advertisement of services, the purpose of which is to identify the services of one person and in so doing, distinguish these services from those of another. For example: marks, names, symbols, titles, slogans, character names, and any distinctive or unique pictures or other advertising used in commerce.

4. *Certification mark*—A certification mark such as "Good Housekeeping Seal of Approval", is used by persons other than the owner of a trademark or service mark to certify that the goods or services meet certain standards; or, have a certain regional origin.

5. *Collective mark*—A collective mark is a trademark or service mark used by the members of a cooperative, an association or other collective group or organization; and includes marks to indicate membership in a union, association or other similar organization—such as, for example, "Third Degree Mason."

*Very Important:* The above and foregoing are protectable business marks. As a legal assistant, it is incumbent upon you to see that any of the above marks are registered immediately. This is because registration under the governing federal act, the "Lanham Act," is prima facie evidence of the exclusive right to the use of the mark; and a strong presumption in favor of the validity of the fact that registration exists (this, together with continued use in commerce for a period of five years or more after its registration). This makes the right to use a mark incontestable and the registration thereof conclusive, rather than presumptive.

# Conclusion

The advent of a legal assistant into the legal work force has proven to be just what the doctor ordered for the organized bar; to assist it in practicing its profession. Utilization of this specially trained individual, has enabled attorneys to lower the cost of the delivery of legal services to the general public, and to do so efficiently.

This is true because the legal assistant does the same thing the attorney would have to do if he did not have a legal assistant—leaving him free to utilize his special attorney skills, i.e., "rainmaking" clients; analysis of facts; judgment ability; planning strategy and advocacy.

And since the trend is for more and more attorneys moving to the use of legal assistants in order to deliver the increasing volume of legal services to our growing, changing society, careful and adequate training of these unique individuals becomes more important.

So now you know how important you are. But remember, to be a viable member of this legal team, you must fully understand what your attorney does in relation to what your functions are as his legal assistant, before you can be an invaluable asset to him in the practice of his profession.

The proper use of this book will give you a head start in this effort. By its daily and careful utilization, you will be able to follow through and complete any legal task assigned by your attorney.

You are, therefore, urged to use this book to avoid disturbing your busy attorney with questions; to enhance your value to your attorney, and to make yourself a truly viable member of the legal team. GOOD LUCK!

# INDEX

# INDEX